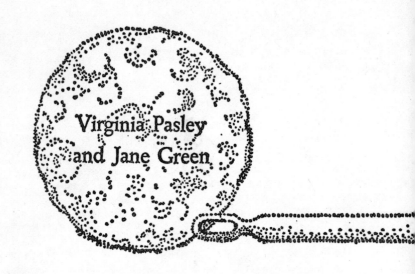

Virginia Pasley
and Jane Green

SIMON AND SCHUSTER
NEW YORK

You Can
Do Anything
with Crepes

For Dan,
For the idea . . .
with love and affection

Contents

A Salute
to the Versatile Crepe

Crepes suffer by their own reputation. Cooks think of them as difficult to make as well as exotic—flaming Crepes Suzette or Delices de Mer—to be used only on very special occasions. The truth is that crepes are easier than pie—and a wonderful asset in any good cook's repertoire.

You Can Do Anything with Crepes

They can be made ahead and frozen. They can be the basis of an elegant party dish for a big crowd, or they can help you create a thrifty family meal incorporating last night's broiled ham or some other tempting tidbits. Crepes fit in at any hour or for any social occasion— from breakfast to bridge parties, from luncheons to late-night snacks. As well as their many main course uses, crepes can be served as hors d'oeuvres or first courses, as vegetable-filled side dishes and as luscious desserts.

Wide Variety, Including Low Calorie

This book includes an unusual range of recipes, many created by the authors to demonstrate the tremendous versatility of crepes. Some of the basic crepe recipes are richer, some are thinner, some have savory seasonings, others are the sweetened dessert type. In our calorie-conscious world, it is happy news that the finest and most delicate crepes are the lowest calorically— about 20 calories each—and the fillings can be low in calories, too: chicken and mushrooms in a clear delicate sauce, tomatoes and cheese, a vegetable mélange, or a sugarless jam or preserve for a dessert filling. There are many such recipes here for fillings, sauces and toppings and a great many suggested variations. And there are at least as many more that could be dreamed up—maybe by you.

Crepes—and Your Imagination

Because crepes freeze superbly, take up little space and defrost in minutes, you can have the makings of an endless variety of delicious dishes on hand for every occasion. Let your imagination explore all the ways this versatile and delicate little pancake can be used to enhance and display even the most ordinary foods. You will be delighted to discover what crepes can do for the sauces and dressings for spaghetti, macaroni and noodles, for most of the accompaniments of rice, for anything that could be served over biscuits or toast points. Most creamed dishes, stews, casseroles and even Chinese stir-fries adapt with but little change to fill a crepe. One idea may lead to another and you may try combining a bit of this recipe with that one. Or best of all you will use just what you have on hand and your own imagination to explore the endless possibilities of crepes.

Crepe Versus Pancake

The basic difference between a crepe and a pancake is that the crepe uses eggs instead of other leavening. It also uses more liquid in proportion to the amount of flour used. A crepe is thin and delicate and is easily rolled around any filling. A pancake uses baking powder or yeast as a leavening agent. It is a thicker and less delicate product and would be almost impossible to roll around a filling.

Crepes Are Easy

Contrary to legend, crepes are not hard to make nor is special equipment necessary. A French crepe pan is nice to have but any small frying pan will work if it is thoroughly cleaned, rinsed and seasoned first. We like to season a pan by heating it until barely hot to the touch, rubbing it with cooking oil and letting it stand overnight. Wipe clean with a paper towel and the pan is ready for use.

For the novice, it is best to start with the less delicate varieties. Don't worry if at first you turn out a few limp or misshapen crepes until you get the hang of it. They will taste just as good as the perfectly round, perfectly browned crepes you will soon be making in no time.

So now—let's make crepes. If you are a beginner, it would be wise to read these detailed directions through carefully before starting. As soon as you have gained a little experience, you can follow the condensed version of the basic crepe recipe on page 23.

Crepes:
Step by Step

*In this section you will find detailed, step-by-step directions
—everything you need to know to make crepes successfully.
How to mix the basic ingredients—by hand, in a mixer or
in a blender. How to choose the right pan. How to cook
crepes; how to turn them (or flip them, if you wish).
Freezing and defrosting filled and unfilled crepes. Assembling stacked crepes.*

BASIC CREPE RECIPE

1½ cups flour
1 teaspoon sugar
⅛ teaspoon salt
3 eggs

1½ cups milk
2 tablespoons butter, or
oil, melted and cooled

Note: This recipe is repeated on page 23 followed by
variations.

Mixing Crepes by Hand

1. Sift the dry ingredients into a bowl.
2. Break the eggs into another bowl and mix until
yolks and whites are blended.
3. Make a hole in the middle of the dry ingredients

and pour in beaten eggs. (French chefs often break the eggs right into the dry ingredients but this makes the mixing more difficult.)

4. Stir the flour mixture into the eggs little by little. The dough will be difficult to work and it may be necessary to add a little milk (or whatever liquid is used in the recipe) to incorporate all the flour. Add the liquid a spoonful at a time and mix it in thoroughly before adding more liquid. When the mixture becomes easy to work (when about half of the liquid has been used) the remainder can be added in two portions.

5. Add melted butter (and flavorings if indicated).

6. Mix again, cover and set aside for at least an hour but not more than 6 hours at room temperature. Crepe batter can be held overnight in the refrigerator. If necessary, the crepe batter can be cooked immediately, but the "resting" time allows the flour to absorb more liquids, makes the batter easier to handle and gives the crepes more flavor. Since flours vary in their ability to absorb liquid, if the crepe batter seems too thick when you are ready to cook it, a small amount of extra liquid can be added at this time. The consistency should be at least as thin as heavy cream.

Mixing Crepes in an Electric Mixer

Beat eggs about a minute at medium speed—until yolks and whites are well blended, add half the dry ingredients and mix until there are no lumps, then add the remaining dry ingredients. If the mixture is too thick for your beaters add a small amount of liquid. Add remaining liquid a little at a time until half is used, then pour in the rest and beat until smooth. Add melted butter and flavorings, beat again, cover and set aside for from 1 to 6 hours. Can be held overnight in the refrigerator.

Mixing Crepes in a Blender

The liquids and eggs should go in first in a blender, including butter and seasonings, then the dry ingredients. Blend for 1 minute, then turn off motor and with a rubber spatula push down flour that has not been blended and blend again for a minute. If necessary repeat until the mixture is well blended. Cover and set aside for 1 to 6 hours at room temperature; can be held overnight in the refrigerator.

Crepe Pans

Any small frying pan can be used, but a French crepe pan with sloping sides makes turning crepes easier. For most recipes, a pan that measures 5 inches across the bottom is a desirable size. We also use a 6-inch pan but prefer the 5-inch size for most recipes. Larger pans are used for special recipes such as stacked crepes. Teflon pans are fine and are especially good for calorie counters.

The pan should be seasoned before use. Heat until just hot to the touch, rub with cooking oil and let it stand overnight. Wipe it clean with a paper towel and the pan is ready for use. Pans that are to be used for crepes should ordinarily not be used for anything else. They become seasoned by use and should never be scoured. They can be wiped clean with paper towels, or at most washed with soap and water.

Cooking Crepes

1. Preheat pan and brush with melted butter.
2. Stir up crepe batter for a moment or two. If it is too thick add a little liquid until batter is the consistency of heavy cream.

3. Use spoon, dipper or ladle that will hold just enough batter for one crepe. When you are expert you may prefer to pour the batter from a pitcher. Experimentation will standardize the amount for you, but a tablespoon and a half is about right for a 5-inch pan; 2 tablespoons for a 6-inch pan.

4. When the butter is hot and bubbling but not brown lift pan off heat and pour in the batter. Quickly tilt the pan so that the batter swirls around and covers the bottom of the pan. If you haven't used enough and there are holes, pour in more.

If you pour in too much the excess can be poured back. The batter that clings to the side of the pan as a result can be cut off after the crepe is cooked.

5. Return pan to heat. If the burner is hot enough and the right amount of batter has been used, the crepe will set almost immediately. When the heat is right it will take about a minute for a plain crepe to brown. Using a round-ended table knife or your fingers, pick up the edge of the crepe and check for browning. Turn up the heat or turn it down if the crepe cooks too slowly or too fast. On electric stoves you may need to alternate between heat 2 and 3. Shake the pan backward, forward and sideways to be sure the crepe does not stick. Then flip it if you wish. Otherwise, with the same round-ended knife, lift up an edge, catch it with your fingers and turn it over. The reverse side will take about a half minute to cook. It will not be as evenly brown as the first side and is always turned inside for filling.

6. Immediately pour in more batter and continue cooking until all the batter is used. Add butter or oil only when pan looks dry, perhaps every second or third crepe. After the first crepe, no butter is needed in no-stick (Teflon) pans.

As each crepe is cooked, turn it out on a clean dish towel or paper towel. If crepes are to be used immediately stack them on a warm plate and keep them in a warm oven until all are made. If they are to be kept a while, stack them after they have cooled with waxed paper between each and keep covered so they do not dry out. If they are to be frozen, wrap the stacked layers in freezer wrap, aluminum foil, or plastic bags and freeze immediately. Be sure to label number and type of crepe packaged. *See* Freezing and Defrosting Crepes, pages 19–20.

Hints on Cooking Crepes

Your first crepe may stick to the pan and tear when you try to turn it. This is either because the pan was not perfectly clean or is not well seasoned. Often the heat is not right for the first crepe and later ones will turn out perfectly. Be patient. Another reason for broken crepes is turning before the crepe has set and browned enough to firm.

If crepes have a hazed or scrambled appearance on the first side, the heat was too high when they were poured in. If they do not brown in a minute or so, the heat is too low. If they are not yet set on top when they are browned on the bottom, too much batter was used. If crepes are too thin on the edges, the batter was swirled too thinly there. However, the edges can be clipped.

Cooking Thin, Delicate or Sweet Crepes

When the proportion of liquid to flour is 2 to 1 or more, the crepes will be thinner and harder to handle. It is particularly important not to touch them until they are well set and browned. Sometimes it will be easier to turn a thin crepe with the help of a narrow flexible metal or plastic spatula, after you have lifted one edge with your fingers. Crepes with a good deal of sugar cook more quickly than plain crepes. They need to be watched carefully or they will get too dark. This is particularly true of the reverse side which may brown in a few seconds.

Cooking Large Crepes

Turning an 8- or 9-inch crepe is much more difficult than turning a 5- or 6-inch crepe. And the difficulties are increased if the batter is thin or sweet. Using a little cream in the batter sometimes helps make the low-flour crepes easier to handle. It is better to use a little more batter proportionately and make a slightly thicker crepe. An 8-inch crepe will require almost three times as much batter as a 5-inch; a 10-inch crepe will require more than four times as much. A wide spatula will help in the turning process. If breaks do occur in turning, a tiny bit of batter can be used to seal the break. We recommend a no-stick pan for cooking the larger crepes.

How to Flip a Crepe

The French usually turn a crepe over by flipping it in the air. Men find this method a lot of fun, and it isn't hard to learn to do it. Here's how: When the first side of the crepe is cooked, shake the pan gently backward and forward and sideways to be sure the crepe is free. Now start shaking it more vigorously and at the same time give the pan a little twisting upward flip. If the crepe doesn't rise out of the pan, flip it a little harder. At first it may only turn over and catch the edge of the pan. Turn it by hand and try again. If you flip it too hard and without the little twist necessary to turn it, the crepe may land on the stove—or even on the floor. Don't be discouraged. After a few casualties you will be flipping with ease for an admiring audience. However we don't recommend flipping the sweet crepes.

Freezing and Defrosting Unfilled Crepes

Wrap the cooked crepes in foil, plastic or freezer wrap in numbers that are most convenient for you to use in a recipe. We wrap the smaller 5-inch crepes in packets of 12, an amount we often use to serve four people 3 crepes per serving.

It is not necessary to have a full-size freezer to be able to freeze crepes. They take up little space and will fit easily into the freezer compartment of a refrigerator.

To defrost crepes, remove outer wrappings and let stand at room temperature. Do not attempt to separate the crepes until they are partially defrosted because they are brittle when frozen and will break easily. When fully defrosted they can be used for any recipe in this book—wrapped around a filling, layered or simmered in a dessert sauce.

Crepes, like most baked goods, can be refrozen. However, crepes that have been frozen too long or refrozen too often tend to become dry and tough. We recommend holding frozen crepes no longer than 2 months and refreezing no more than twice.

Freezing and Defrosting Filled Crepes

Crepes may be filled, put in the casserole, ramekin or disposable aluminum pans in which they are to be baked, wrapped in aluminum foil, freezer paper or plastic freezer bags and frozen. This, of course, will take up more freezer space. They can be frozen with or without a top sauce. Fillings, or in some cases just the basic ingredients for fillings, can be frozen separately, defrosted and combined with the defrosted crepes. They are then treated the same way as freshly made filled crepes.

Frozen filled crepes that have been at room temperature for about an hour will usually require an additional hour for baking. Before putting them in the oven, they may be dotted with butter or cheese or a top sauce may be poured over them. If you wish to defrost them fully before baking, the time of baking will of course be cut to the same 5 to 30 minutes that freshly made crepes require in the oven.

Stacked Main Course Crepes

Instead of rolling each crepe around a filling, crepes can be stacked in layers with fillings in between. Two or more different fillings can be used, although the fillings should have some affinity for each other. (See suggested Fillings for Stacked Crepes, below.) For stacking, you will need to make a larger size crepe—in a 7-, 8- or 9-inch pan. These are harder to handle in the pan and we recommend using the basic crepe recipe or tomato crepes or avocado crepes until you are expert at handling the more delicate batters. For information on cooking larger crepes, see page 18.

Assembling Stacked Crepes

Use a pie plate or low round casserole, slightly larger than the circumference of the crepe. Grease the dish and place one crepe on it. Spread the crepe with filling, not more than a half inch thick. Top with another crepe and spread a different filling. Put on a third crepe and another filling. You can go on with up to five fillings, but more than that makes the stacked crepes difficult to cut. Top with a crepe and either pour over a sauce or sprinkle with cheese or bread crumbs or grated almonds and bake at 375° F. for about 20 minutes. Bring to the table in the baking dish and cut in wedges like a pie and serve with a pie or cake server. If this is assembled with warm crepes, it may go straight to the table without extra baking.

Fillings for Stacked Crepes

1. Pizza fillings. Top with tomato and cheese.
2. Spinach fillings combined with chicken or seafood fillings.
3. Mushroom fillings combined with chicken or seafood fillings.
4. Cannelloni fillings combined with pizza fillings.
5. Spaghetti sauce filling combined with pizza or cannelloni fillings.

Note: Chinese-type fillings are not advisable for stacking.

Basic Crepes
for Main Courses
and Desserts

BASIC CREPES

1½ cups flour
1 teaspoon sugar
⅛ teaspoon salt
3 eggs

1½ cups milk
2 tablespoons butter or
    oil, melted and cooled
butter for cooking

Sift flour, sugar and salt together in a bowl. Add eggs and mix together thoroughly—mixture will form a thick paste. Add milk gradually, beating thoroughly. Add melted and cooled butter. At this time add whatever flavoring you wish and, if possible, allow batter to stand for at least 1 hour. (For more detailed directions on mixing ingredients by hand, or with an electric mixer or blender, see pages 13–15.)

Heat a small crepe pan, 5 or 6 inches across the bottom. Brush with butter or oil and when fat is hot but not smoking lift pan off heat and pour in 1½ to 2 tablespoons of batter, depending on the size of the pan. Swirl quickly to cover bottom of pan. Return pan to heat. When crepe is golden brown (about a minute) turn it and cook on reverse side for about half a minute. Continue cooking crepes, adding butter to pan as needed. Turn crepes out on a clean towel or paper towels. If they are to be used immediately, stack on a plate and keep warm in a low oven. If they are to be held, stack with waxed paper between each after they have cooled and cover. If they are to be frozen, wrap stack in foil, freezer paper or freezer bags and freeze immediately.

Yield: 28–32 5-inch crepes or 16–20 6-inch crepes.

These all-purpose crepes are easy to make and are recommended to the novice. They are neither as tender nor as delicate as recipes with more liquid nor as light as those with more eggs.

This recipe is easily divided into a smaller amount, especially suitable for a meal for two persons. The proportions are: 1 egg, ½ cup flour and ½ cup of liquid, 2 teaspoons butter, ⅓ teaspoon sugar, a pinch of salt.

FLAVORINGS FOR MAIN COURSE CREPES
1 tablespoon brandy
1 tablespoon fresh or 1 teaspoon dried herbs
1 teaspoon grated lemon rind

FLAVORINGS FOR DESSERT CREPES
1 teaspoon vanilla and 1 extra tablespoon sugar
1 tablespoon brandy and 1 extra tablespoon sugar
1 tablespoon Cointreau
1 teaspoon grated lemon rind and 1 extra tablespoon sugar

How to Vary the Basic Crepe Recipe—
or Invent Your Own Crepe Recipe

There are any number of variations possible on the basic crepe proportions. It is possible to give a limited number in this book. There are also many possible flavors and combinations of flavors. Once you master the basic crepe recipe it is not a bit difficult to put together a recipe that is all your own.

Start with the basic proportions of 1 egg, ½ cup of flour and ½ cup of liquid. This is the most flour and the least liquid that will give you a true crepe. More flour and less liquid will get away from the thin crepe and into the thick pancake class. However, you can try less flour and more liquid. You can increase the number of eggs, but not so much that you end up with an omelet instead of a crepe. The liquid doesn't need to be milk; it can be broth or tomato juice or cream or part water.

If you are counting calories you won't put butter in your crepes and you will bake them in a Teflon pan. But a little butter adds to the flavor and the more butter in the crepe—up to a tablespoon for the proportions of 1 egg, ½ cup flour and ½ cup liquid—the less you will need for cooking in a regular crepe pan or ordinary small frying pan. Also a small amount of sugar helps both flavor and browning.

For flavor and textures you can add brandy which will also make the crepes lighter; herbs, cayenne or curry powder for main course crepes. For dessert crepes, try experimenting with sweet liqueurs, vanilla or cocoa. Grated orange or lemon rind can be used for either main course or dessert crepes to enhance flavor. For both texture and flavor, cheese can be added, or finely grated nuts.

A dessert recipe given in this book (page 33) includes sour cream. If you devise a recipe with sour cream you will find that it will make too thick a pancake unless other liquid is added. More liquid is needed also when a thick puree is added such as the mashed avocado in Avocado Crepes (page 27). Crepes made with water or broth are more delicate and harder to handle than those made with milk. A little cream—1 tablespoon or so—makes it possible to cut down the amount of flour and have a delicate crepe that is easy to handle.

EXTRA RICH CREPES

4 eggs	1 tablespoon brandy
½ cup flour	¼ teaspoon sugar
1 cup cream	¼ teaspoon salt

Combine ingredients and cook like Basic Crepes, page 23.
Yield: 28–34 5-inch crepes or 16–18 6-inch crepes.

EXTRA THIN CREPES

3 eggs	2 cups milk (or half milk
¾ cup flour	and half cream)
1 tablespoon brandy	2 tablespoons butter,
½ teaspoon sugar	melted and cooled (if
¼ teaspoon salt	all milk is used)

Combine ingredients and cook like Basic Crepes, page 23.
Yield: 28–34 5-inch crepes or 16–18 6-inch crepes.

SOUFFLÉED CREPES

3 eggs, separated
1 cup milk
¾ cup flour
½ teaspoon sugar

¼ teaspoon salt
2 tablespoons butter,
  melted and cooled

These proportions make an eggier-tasting crepe. Beat
the egg yolks with part of the milk, add flour, sugar
and salt, beat well. Add remaining milk gradually, then
melted butter. Beat egg whites stiff. Fold into crepe
mixture. They either may be cooked in the usual way
in a crepe pan or put into a large buttered pan and
baked in a preheated 375° F. oven for about 25–30
minutes. This then becomes something like a flat soufflé that can be topped with a filling or one can be
put over half the batter, the rest poured on top. It can
be a sweet filling like strawberries or apples and may be
flavored with lemon rind, brandy, or vanilla.

AVOCADO CREPES

½ cup mashed and sieved
  ripe avocado
3 eggs
¾ cup flour
1½ cups milk

1 teaspoon sugar
salt and pepper
1 teaspoon butter, melted
  and cooled

These crepes are best made in a blender. Put in the
avocado and eggs first, then add all the rest of the

ingredients. Cook according to directions for Basic Crepes (page 23). Easy to make in larger sizes.
Yield: 28–34 5-inch crepes or 16–18 6-inch crepes.

ALTERNATE FLAVORINGS
1 teaspoon grated lemon rind is a good addition. Herbs such as a tablespoon of chopped parsley or ½ teaspoon of thyme may be added, as well as a few grates of fresh nutmeg.

SUGGESTED USES
With seafood fillings, especially crabmeat
With chicken fillings

CHEESE CREPES

3 eggs
1 cup flour
1 teaspoon sugar
pinch of salt
½ cup grated cheese
  (Parmesan or Gruyere
  or a mixture of both)

1½ cups milk or part milk
  and part chicken stock
2 tablespoons butter,
  melted and cooled

Beat eggs, blend into flour, sugar and salt. The dough will be stiff and if the eggs are small, a little of the liquid may have to be added. Beat in the grated cheese which should be as finely grated as possible, then add liquid in small amounts, beating in between until mixture is smooth.

Cook according to directions for Basic Crepes, page 23.
Yield: 28–34 5-inch crepes or 16–18 6-inch crepes.

ALTERNATE SEASONINGS

Add herbs of your choice; a tablespoon of chopped parsley, a half teaspoon each of basil, thyme, or oregano. Or add 1 tablespoon brandy. You may also add 1½ teaspoons of Italian Seasoning.

SUGGESTED USES

With pizza fillings
With cannelloni fillings
With chicken, mushroom and ham fillings
For any crepe recipe with Mornay sauce

TOMATO CREPES

3 eggs	*½ cup water or stock*
1 cup flour	*salt and pepper to taste*
½ teaspoon sugar	*2 tablespoons butter,*
1 cup tomato juice	*melted and cooled*

Beat eggs and add flour and sugar. Add tomato juice and water or stock, salt and pepper and melted, cooled butter. Bake according to directions for Basic Crepes, page 23.

If tomato juice is particularly thick, use half tomato juice and half water.

Yield: 28–34 5-inch crepes or 16–18 6-inch crepes.

VARIATIONS

Up to ½ cup of grated Swiss or Parmesan cheese may be added. Herbs of your choice, about ½ teaspoon such as basil or oregano, may be added.

SUGGESTED USES
In any recipes with tomato sauce such as pizza crepes
or crepes with spaghetti sauce

LOW CALORIE CREPES (20 CALORIES EACH)

2 eggs
½ cup flour
½ teaspoon sugar
1 cup broth, stock
  or consommé (fat free)

1 tablespoon chopped
  parsley or herbs of your
  choice

Beat eggs slightly, add flour and sugar and beat until
well mixed. Add chicken broth gradually, beating after
each addition. Butter a small crepe pan or frying pan,
heat until butter is bubbling, and pour about a tablespoon and a half of batter in, swirling it around so that
the batter covers the pan. Cook on one side about a
minute, until brown; turn crepe over and cook on the
other side about a half a minute. Use with any first
course or main course filling.
Yield: 16–20 5-inch crepes, 20 calories per crepe.

Note: These crepes may be cooked in a Teflon pan
without butter.

SUGGESTED USES
Especially suitable with any of the Chinese-type fillings
With green onions, bacon and cheese

BASIC DESSERT CREPES

2 eggs	1 tablespoon brandy
¾ cup flour	1 tablespoon butter,
2 tablespoons sugar	melted and cooled
1 cup milk	

Beat eggs and add flour and sugar, with a little milk if
paste is too thick. Add remaining milk, brandy and
melted and cooled butter. Allow to stand for at least
1 hour.

Butter a 5-inch crepe pan and heat until butter bubbles. Pour in about 1½ tablespoons of batter, swirling
it swiftly around the pan so the bottom is covered.
Cook until light brown on one side—about a minute—
turn crepe over and cook on the other side for about
half a minute. Turn out on paper towels or a tea towel.
If crepes are not to be used immediately, stack with
waxed paper in between.

To freeze, put in freezer bags and seal. To defrost,
set at room temperature for a short time. They will
defrost more quickly if they are separated. But be careful, as crepes are brittle and will crack easily in the
frozen state. They can be refrozen and defrosted again
without harm.

Yield: 28–34 5-inch crepes or 16–18 6-inch crepes.

DESSERT CREPES I

3 eggs
2 tablespoons sugar
1 cup flour
1½ cups milk, or part milk
and part water
2 tablespoons butter,
melted and cooled

pinch of salt
1 tablespoon brandy,
or liqueur
or ½ teaspoon vanilla

Combine ingredients and cook like Basic Dessert Crepes, page 31.

DESSERT CREPES II

3 eggs
¼ cup sugar
¾ cup flour
1½ cups milk or part
cream and part milk
2 tablespoons butter,
melted and cooled

pinch of salt
1 tablespoon brandy
or liqueur or
½ teaspoon vanilla or
1 teaspoon grated
lemon rind

Combine ingredients and cook like Basic Dessert Crepes, page 31.

DESSERT CREPES WITH SOUR CREAM

3 eggs
¼ cup light brown sugar
¾ cup flour

1 cup milk
½ cup sour cream
salt

Combine ingredients and cook like Basic Dessert Crepes, page 31.

SWEET SOUFFLÉED BAKED CREPES

(This recipe is for oven baking only.)

4 eggs, separated
1 cup milk
½ cup flour
½ cup sugar

¼ teaspoon salt
½ cup cream
2 tablespoons butter,
* melted and cooled*

Beat the egg yolks with half of the milk. Add flour, sugar and salt; beat well. The mixture will be stiff. Add remaining milk and cream gradually, then melted butter. Beat egg whites stiff. Fold into crepe mixture. Bake in 2 8-inch-round baking pans, buttered and preheated, in a 375° F. oven for 25–30 minutes.

Serve with precooked sliced and sweetened apples, rhubarb, strawberries, blueberries or what have you, which may be added after baking or before (in which case they will sink into the batter for a different but delicious result).

Cocoa Crepes

2 eggs
½ cup flour
2 tablespoons cocoa
¼ cup sugar

1 cup milk with a little
cream
1 teaspoon vanilla
1 tablespoon butter,
melted and cooled

Put all ingredients into a blender and blend for about 30 seconds at half speed. Or mix eggs and flour by hand or in a mixer adding cocoa and sugar and then milk gradually, beating all the time. Add vanilla and cooled, melted butter and beat once more. Let stand covered an hour or two.

Heat a small skillet or crepe pan—about 5 inches in diameter, brush with butter and when butter bubbles up, pour about a tablespoon and a half of crepe batter into pan, swirling so batter covers the pan. Cook for about 1 minute, check for browning and watch carefully—both the cocoa and the sugar cause crepes to burn easily. Turn crepe over and cook for about a half minute on the other side. Turn out on paper towels.

This recipe will make from 18–24 crepes depending on the size of the pan and amount of batter used for each crepe. These freeze well.

Variations
Add ½ cup finely grated almonds, walnuts or hazelnuts to the batter just before cooking the crepes.

Or add 1–2 tablespoons of crème de cacao to the batter and mix well.

SUGGESTED USES

Cocoa crepes go well with many of the dessert crepe fillings, especially pastry cream, whipped cream, ice cream, apricots, sugar and nuts.

Hors d'Oeuvre
and First Course
Crepes

There are many ways of using crepes as hors d'oeuvres or for first courses. Many of the main course crepes in this book, especially the fish and seafood crepes, make elegant first courses. A traditional first course are Blini, the Russian version of crepes (page 43) with caviar or smoked salmon. And, less well known, crepes can be cut in strips and used instead of noodles in clear soup. We have devised some new ways of using crepes as hors d'oeuvres: as tarts for quichetype fillings, as coverings for Chinese egg rolls, and, crisped in the oven, as a base for spreads or dips.

CONSOMMÉ CELESTINE

4 cups chicken broth   a few fresh spinach leaves
½ chicken breast   or slivered green beans
4 or 5 crepes

If using homemade chicken broth, clarify (whip one egg white with its broken shell, add it to boiling broth; continue to boil for 10 minutes, then strain through cheesecloth). Cut cooked crepes (any main course recipe or the special one that follows) into long thin strips. This is a good way to use misshapen crepes. Cut uncooked breast of chicken into match-stick strips and cook for 2 or 3 minutes in the simmering broth. Then add crepes and finally the raw spinach or slivered green beans. Cook 1 minute more. Check for seasoning and serve. Serves 4 if main course is light, 6 before a substantial meal.

CREPES FOR CONSOMMÉ CELESTINE

2 eggs
¼ cup flour
2 tablespoons finely grated almonds
1 tablespoon finely chopped parsley

¾ cup milk or chicken broth
1 tablespoon butter, melted and cooled
1 teaspoon brandy
pinch of salt

Combine eggs and flour, add grated almonds and parsley. Stir in milk or broth gradually and beat until smooth. Add melted butter, brandy and salt. Let stand for 2 hours.

Butter a crepe pan or skillet. Since there crepes are delicate and hard to turn, a small pan is easier. Brush the pan with melted butter and when the butter bubbles up and is almost sizzling, pour in a little batter. Swirl pan so that the batter coats it and cook about a minute until lightly browned on one side. Turn with fingers or a spatula and cook about a half minute on other side. As each crepe is baked turn out on a towel. When cool, cut in strips.

BEEF BOUILLON WITH CREPES

4 cups clarified brown
    stock or beef bouillon
slivered raw beef or
    leftover rare steak or
    roast beef (about ¼
    pound)

4 or 5 crepes
1 finely chopped
    peeled tomato

Bring the clarified stock (follow directions for clarifying chicken stock page 37) or the beef bouillon to a boil. Add paper-thin shreds of beef and simmer for a minute or two, then add the crepes cut in strips. Use any main course crepes or special Crepes for Consommé Celestine, substituting beef broth for chicken broth and omitting grated almonds. Add the chopped tomato and serve at once.

ONION SOUP WITH CREPES

Instead of toast or bread, use crepes cut into noodle strips. Put the crepe strips on top of the soup in individual heatproof bowls and sprinkle with cheese. Run under broiler for 3 or 4 minutes until cheese bubbles and browns slightly.

CREPE EGG ROLLS WITH CHICKEN

1 cup cooked chicken
1 thin slice prosciutto
or boiled ham
1 tablespoon peanut oil
2 tablespoons chopped
scallion or onion
2 tablespoons chopped
celery

1 cup bean sprouts or
mixed Chinese vege-
tables frozen or canned
1 teaspoon soy sauce
salt if needed
12 main course crepes
(page 49)
oil for frying

Chicken wings and backs can be used in this recipe. The chicken should be cut in fine julienne strips, as should the ham. Heat the oil in a skillet and add the scallion or onion and the chopped celery and cook for only a minute or two. Add the bean sprouts or Chinese vegetables, chicken, ham and sprinkle the soy sauce over all, stirring to heat and blend for just a minute or so. Check for seasoning; salt may not be needed because of the ham and soy sauce.

It is inadvisable to use the more delicate crepes for this recipe. If you are making crepes specially, do not let the second side brown. Put a tablespoon of filling in the center of each crepe on the second side. Fold up one end of the crepe and then fold over the two sides, as though you were making an envelope. Use crepe batter or beaten egg to hold the fold in place. Then fold over the top to complete the envelope and anchor with batter or beaten egg. Let stand a few minutes, then fry in about a half inch of oil, turning so all sides get brown. Handle carefully when turning and brown only lightly. Transfer to a rack on a shallow pan and finish crisping in a 400° F. oven for about 15 minutes. Let stand 5 minutes before serving with cocktail napkins.

VARIATIONS

Use 1 cup of chopped cooked shrimp instead of chicken. Mix 2 teaspoons of sherry with the soy sauce and sprinkle over the mixture.

Use 1 cup of crabmeat instead of chicken. Omit ham. Mix ½ teaspoon dry mustard with 1 tablespoon sherry and sprinkle over mixture.

CREPES FOR DIPS AND SPREADS

Use any of the main course crepes for these. If you use the basic crepe recipe, add a little more liquid; since the crepes are cooked differently they are likely to be too thick unless this is done. Use a large skillet or griddle, butter it and heat until butter bubbles. From a spoon or dipper, pour a small amount of batter—about half a tablespoon to make a 2- to 3-inch crepe. Do not tilt the pan and pour steadily into the center. The crepes will not be perfectly even, but any unsightly knobs can be cut off. Turn crepe when brown on one side and brown on the other. Four or five can be cooked at the same time, pouring a new one whenever there is room. A 3-egg recipe will make dozens of these little crepes.

Crepes can be made early in the day—or cooked and frozen days earlier. They then will need to be crisped in the oven. To do this set oven at about 350° F. Spread crepes over a cookie sheet and bake about 15 minutes, turning once. Serve them with any preferred dip, with soft cheese or thin pieces of hard cheese. Many of the hors d'oeuvre and main course fillings can also be served with the small crepes.

CREPES WITH DEVILED CRAB SPREAD

½ pound crabmeat, shredded

2 tablespoons butter

2 tablespoons minced green onions

2 tablespoons minced green pepper

2 tablespoons minced celery

2 teaspoons cornstarch

½ cup heavy cream

2 egg yolks

1 teaspoon prepared mustard

½ teaspoon dry mustard

1 teaspoon Worcestershire sauce

½ teaspoon paprika

salt, black and cayenne pepper to taste

4 8-inch avocado crepes (page 27) or 8 6-inch crepes

Canned crabmeat is fine for this and is easier to shred, which is necessary in order to get a spreading consistency. Melt the butter in a medium-sized skillet and sauté the minced onions, green pepper and celery until wilted—about 5 minutes. Blend the cornstarch into the cream, add the egg yolks and beat well, then mix in the mustards, Worcestershire sauce, paprika, salt, black pepper to taste and a little cayenne if a hotter taste is desired. Add the crabmeat to the vegetables and cook for a minute or two over high heat to evaporate some of the juice which will come out of the crabmeat. Turn down the heat and add the cream-egg yolk mixture, stirring thoroughly. The final mixture should be thick.

Spread two of the 8-inch or four of the 6-inch crepes with the crab and top with the remaining crepes. Place on a cookie sheet and bake at 400° F. for about 20 minutes. Slide onto a serving plate and cut into wedges. Serve with cocktail napkins.

BLINI (BUCKWHEAT CREPES)

1 cup milk
½ package yeast
4 eggs, separated
½ teaspoon salt

1 teaspoon sugar
3 tablespoons melted
butter
1½ cups sifted buckwheat flour

Scald milk and let it cool until lukewarm. Add the yeast and stir until dissolved. Beat the egg yolks until thick and creamy. Add the yeast mixture, the salt, sugar, melted butter and buckwheat flour. This mixture must rise until double in bulk, approximately 1–1½ hours. Beat the egg whites until stiff, and gently fold them into the batter.

Preheat and lightly butter a griddle. Using only 1 tablespoon of batter, cook the blini until golden on one side, turning once. Keep the griddle lightly buttered. This recipe should make approximately 30 blini. They do *not* freeze well.

SUGGESTIONS FOR SERVING

BLINI WITH CAVIAR
Serve the above blini with spoonfuls of caviar, chopped hard-cooked egg white and sieved hard-cooked egg yolk and finely chopped onion.

BLINI WITH SMOKED SALMON
Serve the above blini with thinly sliced smoked salmon and capers; sour cream may also be served if desired.

CREPES QUICHE WITH BACON

8 ounces cream cheese
½ cup heavy cream
1 egg
1 egg yolk
black pepper
2 tablespoons chopped
  chives

4 tablespoons grated
  sharp cheddar cheese
  (Herkimer County)
6 strips of cooked and
  crumbled bacon
18 5-inch crepes

Let cream cheese stand at room temperature for an hour before starting. Then cream in gradually the cream, then the whole egg and the egg yolk until the mixture is smooth and thick. Add black pepper, chives and grated cheese, mixing well.

Have ready 3 muffin tins each with 6 muffin cups (2½ inches in diameter). Do not grease. Place a crepe over one opening; then put a few bits of cooked bacon and a large spoonful of the cheese mixture in the center and push down carefully with the bowl of a spoon. Repeat with the rest of the crepes. The crepes will make a pastrylike shell around the edge of the filling. Bake for 30 minutes in a 375° F. oven. These may be half baked, frozen and re-baked after defrosting.

CREPES QUICHE WITH HAM

Cut a ¼ pound of ham into small cubes and put it on the center of the crepes before adding the cheese mixture.

CREPES QUICHE WITH CRABMEAT

Add 4 ounces of crabmeat to the cheese mixture, mixing lightly. Use canned, fresh or frozen.

CREPES QUICHE WITH ONION

Cook a cup of finely chopped onions in 4 tablespoons of butter, watching so that it does not burn. Season with a little salt, ¼ teaspoon nutmeg, and a drop of Tabasco sauce. Cook until the onions are very soft. Add to the cheese mixture and cook as above.

CREPES QUICHE WITH CLAMS

Drain the liquid from a 6-ounce can of chopped clams and add to the cheese mixture along with 2 more tablespoons of chives and a speck of hot pepper.

CREPES QUICHE WITH LOBSTER

Sauté half a cup of finely chopped celery in a table-spoon of butter for 3 or 4 minutes. Add 4 to 6 ounces of lobster to the pan, season to taste and combine with the cheese mixture.

CREPES FILLED WITH CHICKEN LIVER PÂTÉ

1 pound chicken livers	½ cup cream
1 pound chicken or turkey giblets	2 eggs
	2 tablespoons brandy
1 tablespoon finely chopped onion	¼ bay leaf
	¼ teaspoon thyme
4 tablespoons butter	1 teaspoon salt
¼ pound mushrooms, chopped	¼ teaspoon black pepper
	18 to 20 crepes
½ cup chicken or giblet stock	melted butter
	½ cup breadcrumbs

Wash and dry livers and remove connective tissue. Clean giblets and precook in water to cover for 20 minutes. Sauté onion in butter until limp, add chicken livers and mushrooms and edible part of precooked giblets. Sauté for 4 or 5 minutes. Put in blender and add stock, cream, eggs, brandy, bay leaf and thyme, salt and pepper. Blend until smooth. Mixture will be liquid. Pour into a bowl and chill until thick. Lacking a blender, use a food chopper to grind livers, giblets, mushrooms, onions and bay leaf with a fine blade, add rest of ingredients and mix thoroughly; chill.

Put 2 spoonfuls along the center of each crepe, roll and turn seam side down in a buttered baking dish. Spread a little melted or softened butter over the crepes, sprinkle with breadcrumbs and bake in a 375° F. oven for 15–20 minutes. This does *not* freeze well but will keep up to a week in the refrigerator if well wrapped in moistureproof wrappings. May be served hot as a first course. Sliced and served cold as an hors d'oeuvre, it will serve 25 or 30.

CREPES WITH CHICKEN LIVERS AND MUSHROOMS

1 pound chicken livers
4 tablespoons butter
1 medium onion, sliced and finely cut
½ pound mushrooms, sliced
salt and pepper to taste
½ cup red wine
½ cup beef stock or bouillon
1 strip orange peel
2 teaspoons cornstarch
16 crepes
½ cup buttered breadcrumbs

Clean chicken livers and cut in pieces. Melt butter in a large skillet and when it bubbles put in onion; cook until limp, then add chicken livers and mushrooms. Allow to brown slightly, add salt and pepper to taste, then red wine and beef stock or bouillon with strip of orange peel. Simmer for about 5 minutes; remove peel. Pour off a little of the juice in the pan, cool and blend with 2 teaspoons of cornstarch. Pour cornstarch mixture into pan and stir until well blended and thick.

Cool slightly, then put a spoonful or two of filling on each crepe, roll and turn seam side down in a buttered baking dish. Sprinkle top with buttered breadcrumbs and bake at 375° F. for 15 minutes. Does *not* freeze well.

Main Course Crepes

The possibilities of fillings for main course crepes are limited only by ingenuity and imagination. A good half of the recipes given here are well adapted to leftovers since they call for precooked meat, chicken or seafood. The recipes themselves are adaptable to your own tastes. Spices or herbs can be omitted or added; though the resulting dish will be different, it isn't likely that it will be harmed. Leftover gravy may be substituted for cream sauce and if the gravy was good in the first place, again no harm will be done. Many of the recipes are elaborate—you wouldn't be reading this book now if all you wanted was another way of using mushroom soup. And some that look elaborate are easy enough to prepare. All of the dishes can be prepared right up to the top sauce and held in the refrigerator for hours. Most can be made ahead and frozen. The really elaborate ones need nothing more to make a perfect meal than a tossed green salad, a plain green vegetable and fruit for dessert.

The recipes that follow are arranged according to the principal ingredient in the filling. There are 12 variations with beef, 7 with veal, 7 with pork, ham or bacon, 5 with lamb, 16 with chicken or turkey, 22 with fish or seafood, 6 versions of pizza crepes and 3 of cannelloni made with crepes.

With Beef Fillings

CREPES WITH STEAK AND SNOW PEAS

1 pound steak	3 tablespoons peanut oil
¼ cup soy sauce	2 packages frozen snow
¼ cup sherry	peas (edible pea pods)
2 teaspoons cornstarch	½ cup chicken broth
1 thinly sliced	or consommé
shredded scallion	16 5-inch crepes

Slice steak into thin strips about ¼ inch thick and an inch wide. Mix soy sauce, sherry, cornstarch and thinly sliced scallion in a bowl and add the steak strips. Marinate about a half hour. Heat 2 tablespoons of the peanut oil in a large skillet over high heat, add the steak mixture and stir with a wooden spoon or fork, swishing the steak all around for a minute or two until it is seared on all sides. Remove from pan and put in the third tablespoon of peanut oil. When it is sizzling hot, drop in the snow peas which have been partially defrosted. Again over high heat stir until all pea pods are separated and beginning to soften. Return steak mixture to pan with pea pods and add ½ cup chicken broth and cook for 2 or 3 minutes. If sauce does not thicken, mix another teaspoon of cornstarch with a little more chicken broth and stir into mixture.

Fill crepes that have been warmed and serve immediately. Or fill crepes, place seam side down in a buttered baking dish and freeze. (See freezing and defrosting instructions, page 19.)

Crepes with Beef and Blue Cheese

1 pound ground beef
  (half chuck and
  half round steak)
½ cup chopped onions
2 tablespoons salad oil
½ cup finely chopped
  black olives

⅓ cup blue cheese
1 cup sour cream
1 egg
salt and pepper to taste
16 5-inch crepes

Brown beef and onions in the oil in a large skillet. Add finely chopped black olives. Crumble blue cheese with a fork and mix it with the sour cream and the egg. Add to the beef mixture in the skillet and cook over low heat for 4 or 5 minutes, stirring constantly. Check for seasoning. No salt may be needed if the blue cheese is salty. Cool.

Butter a baking pan. Put a spoonful or two of the beef mixture along the center of each crepe, fold and roll. Turn seam side down. Brush the tops of the crepes with butter and bake at 375° F. for 20 minutes. May be frozen and baked the same as when freshly made if completely defrosted. If in a freezer-to-oven pan, they then should be baked at 300° F. for 40 minutes and at 375° F. for 15 minutes.

CREPES WITH BEEF AND ARTICHOKES GREEK STYLE

1 pound ground beef
(half chuck and
half round steak)
1 cup finely chopped
onions
2 tablespoons olive oil
salt and pepper to taste
½ teaspoon oregano
½ teaspoon nutmeg
grated rind of 1 lemon
1 large tomato, cut
in small pieces
1 package frozen arti-
choke hearts, defrosted
½ cup beef stock
or bouillon

½ cup cream
2 tablespoons grated
Parmesan cheese
16 5-inch crepes
Sauce:
1 tablespoon cornstarch
1 cup milk
½ cup cream
1 egg
2 egg yolks
½ teaspoon nutmeg
½ cup grated
Parmesan cheese

Brown the ground beef and the chopped onions in the olive oil. Add salt and pepper to taste, along with oregano, nutmeg, grated rind of lemon and the cut-up tomato. Cut the defrosted artichoke hearts into pieces, about a half inch square. Add to meat mixture with beef stock or bouillon. Mix in 2 tablespoons of Parmesan cheese and cream beaten with the egg. Cool.

Butter a large baking pan and fill each crepe with a spoonful or two of the mixture, roll up and turn seam side down. Mix the cornstarch with a little of the milk in a saucepan and add the rest of the milk and the cream. Bring to a boil and simmer for 3 or 4 minutes.

Beat whole egg and egg yolks together lightly. Remove the sauce from the heat and mix in the egg mixture thoroughly. Mix in half the grated cheese. Pour over the crepes, sprinkle the rest of the cheese on top and bake for 40 minutes at 350° F. Let stand 15 minutes before serving.

It is better to freeze this dish without the sauce, defrost it completely and then put the sauce over and finish it like the freshly made dish.

CREPES WITH BEEF AND BEAN SPROUTS

1½ pounds flank steak
1 one-pound can bean
   sprouts
4 tablespoons butter
1 green pepper, cut in
   chunks

1 cup beef or chicken
   stock
4 tablespoons soy sauce
14–16 5-inch crepes

Slice steak in paper-thin slices and then into bite-size pieces. Rinse and drain bean sprouts. Sauté steak quickly in butter until well browned, but do not overcook. Add the green pepper, beef or chicken stock and soy sauce. Cook together quickly until steak is just done.

Place a spoonful or two of mixture down the center of each crepe. Roll and turn seam side down in a buttered baking dish. Any liquid that remains in the pan may be poured over the crepes before baking. Bake at 375° F. for 20 minutes. May be frozen. To serve, defrost first and then bake the same as when freshly made.

CREPES WITH BEEF STROGANOFF

1½ pounds of boneless
 sirloin
4 tablespoons butter
1 large sweet onion,
 chopped
½ pound mushrooms,
 chopped
½ cup beef stock or
 bouillon

1 cup sour cream
1 teaspoon dry mustard
2 tablespoons catsup
1 teaspoon Worcestershire
 sauce
salt and pepper to taste
14–16 5-inch crepes
sour cream for topping
 (optional)

Cut the sirloin into thin slices and then cut the slices into small pieces. Melt butter in a large saucepan and when it bubbles put in the onion and cook for about 5 minutes. Turn up the heat and add steak and cook until it no longer shows pink. Add the mushrooms and cook 3 or 4 minutes longer. Then add beef stock and simmer for another 2 or 3 minutes. Mix the mustard, catsup and Worcestershire sauce into the sour cream and stir into the meat mixture on low heat. Check seasoning.

Put a spoonful or two of the mixture down the center of each crepe. Roll and turn seam side down in a buttered baking dish. Top with more sour cream if desired and bake at 375° F. for 20 minutes. This freezes well. To serve, defrost completely and bake the same as when freshly made.

CREPES WITH CHILI

2 tablespoons cooking oil

1 small onion, chopped fine

1 pound ground beef

1 cup tomato sauce

1–2 tablespoons chili powder

2 tablespoons grated cheese (cheddar or American)

salt and pepper to taste

1 small can pinto or kidney beans

14–16 5-inch crepes

for garnish: chopped onions, chopped tomatoes, shredded lettuce and grated cheddar or American cheese

Heat the oil in a large skillet and add the finely chopped onion. Cook over medium heat until the onion wilts. Add the ground beef and stir and cook until no red shows. Add the tomato sauce and simmer for half an hour. Add the chili powder and simmer another 20 minutes. Then add the cheese and taste for seasoning. Add one small can of beans. Cool.

Oil a large baking pan. Put two spoonfuls of mixture along the center of each crepe. Do not roll. As you fill each crepe push it close to the last one so the rounded edges of the crepes stand up. Bake in a 350° F. oven for about 30 minutes until edges of crepes are crisp and brown. Serve with chopped onions, tomatoes and shredded lettuce or grated cheese. These garnishes can be passed in bowls or served from the kitchen on each plate along with the chili crepes. Serve two to a person and allow one extra apiece for seconds.

This recipe can be frozen baked or unbaked but will need to be placed on the top layer in your freezer so that the tops of the crepes are not broken. If prebaked allow to defrost thoroughly before baking and bake 15 minutes at 375° F.

This recipe came from Mrs. Andrew Mitchell, one of the fine cooks of Rogers, Arkansas, where Southwest cooking is popular. Mrs. Mitchell uses tacos for her chili, but crepes can very well be substituted.

CREPES WITH BEEF IN BURGUNDY

1½ pounds lean beef from round or sirloin
⅛ pound salt pork
2 tablespoons butter
1 small can tiny onions
1 cup red wine
1 cup beef stock or canned bouillon

2 strips orange peel
½ teaspoon thyme
salt and pepper to taste
½ pound mushrooms, quartered
2 tablespoons flour
14–16 5-inch crepes

Cut the beef into bite-size pieces. Dice the salt pork and fry in the butter in a large skillet. When brown, remove and set aside. Drain the onions and fry in the butter and pork fat until golden. Set aside. Over high heat brown the meat on all sides. Heat the wine and the bouillon and add to the meat along with the browned salt pork, orange peel and thyme. Salt and pepper to taste and simmer covered for about 2 hours. Add the browned onions and the quartered mushrooms—they may be sautéed in butter first for added richness. Pour a little of the pan juices into a cup, cool slightly and stir in the flour. Return the flour mixture to the pan and cook until mixture thickens.

Butter a baking dish. Put a spoonful or two of the

mixture down the center of each crepe. Roll and turn seam side down in the baking dish. If some of the sauce is left, spread it over the tops of the crepes. Or brush the tops with butter or buttered crumbs. Bake at 375° F. for 20 minutes. This does *not* freeze well.

CREPES WITH CREAMED DRIED BEEF

5-ounce jar dried beef　　*2 eggs*
2 tablespoons butter　　*9 or 10 5-inch crepes*
2 tablespoons flour
1 cup milk (or part
　milk and part cream)

Separate and shred dried beef. Heat butter in skillet and add dried beef, stirring until all the meat is coated with butter. Add flour and stir again over medium heat until browning starts. Add milk (or milk and cream) all at once to beef mixture and continue stirring until sauce thickens—3 or 4 minutes. Break eggs into creamed beef, stirring rapidly until eggs are well amalgamated. Part of the egg will thicken the sauce and part will scramble—this is the desired effect.

Put a couple of spoonfuls of creamed beef on each crepe which has been warmed and serve immediately. Or place each crepe seam side down in a buttered baking dish and heat for 5 or 10 minutes in a 375° F. oven. These may be frozen and reheated the same as freshly made after defrosting.

CREPES WITH MEATBALLS IN TOMATO SAUCE

1 pound ground round
steak
1 small onion, chopped
4 medium-sized mush-
rooms, chopped
1 tablespoon butter
2 tablespoons chicken
broth (or cream)
1 egg
1 tablespoon grated Par-
mesan or Romano
cheese

1 teaspoon salt
¼ teaspoon pepper
½ teaspoon basil
¼ teaspoon oregano
1 tablespoon butter
14–16 5-inch crepes
2 cups tomato sauce
(page 175)
½ cup grated cheese

Put ground round steak in a bowl. Sauté chopped onion and mushrooms in one tablespoon of butter until
limp. Add 2 tablespoons of chicken broth or cream
and remove from heat. Pour over meat in bowl; mix
thoroughly. Then beat in egg, grated cheese and seasonings.

Form the meat into small balls of about a teaspoon
each and sauté in the second tablespoon of butter for
about 10 minutes, shaking the pan and turning the
meatballs so they are browned on all sides.

Butter a baking pan or bake in individual casseroles
—3 to a serving. Put 4 or 5 small meatballs in the center
of each crepe, spoon tomato sauce over the meatballs,
fold and pour any remaining tomato sauce over the
top, but do *not* turn seam side down. Sprinkle with
grated cheese and bake for about 15 minutes in a
400° F. oven. If cheese does not bubble or brown, slip

under broiler for a minute or two. This freezes well. Defrost completely and bake the same as freshly made.

Crepes with Meat Spaghetti Sauce

3 medium sized tomatoes,
   peeled
1 15-ounce can tomato
   juice
1 clove garlic, peeled
1 grated onion
1 small bay leaf
½ teaspoon oregano

½ teaspoon basil
pinch of rosemary
2 tablespoons olive
   or salad oil
¾ pound ground lean beef
14–16 5-inch crepes
grated Parmesan or
   Romano cheese

Cut tomatoes into small pieces. Add tomato juice, garlic clove, grated onion, bay leaf and herbs. Cook over medium heat for 15 or 20 minutes or until tomatoes are soft. The tomatoes and seasonings may be whirred in the blender for 30 seconds.

Heat the oil in a large skillet and brown the ground beef for 4 or 5 minutes over high heat, stirring continuously. Add the tomato sauce to the meat and stir and cook until well thickened.

Butter or oil a baking dish. Put a spoonful or two of the filling along the center of each crepe, roll and turn seam side down. Sprinkle the tops of the crepes with grated Parmesan or Romano cheese. Or spread extra tomato sauce or tomato juice over the tops and then sprinkle with cheese. Bake in a 400° F. oven for 15 minutes. These may be frozen with or without sauce, defrosted and baked the same as freshly made. Or in a freezer-to-oven pan, bake for 40 minutes at 300° F. then 15 minutes at 400° F.

CREPES WITH SPANISH BEEF STEW

1½ pounds lean beef
4 tablespoons olive oil
1 onion, peeled and
  coarsely chopped
1 whole clove garlic,
  peeled
1 tomato, peeled and
  coarsely chopped
½ cup red wine
1 tablespoon flour

½ teaspoon thyme
¼ teaspoon cloves
½ cup boiling stock or
  water
1 tablespoon minced
  parsley
1 cup cooked peas
  or artichoke hearts
salt and pepper to taste
14–16 5-inch crepes

Cut the beef into small bite-size pieces. Heat 2 tablespoons of the olive oil in a heavy pan and brown the meat on all sides. Remove from pan. Add the rest of the oil and brown the onion and garlic. Add chopped tomato and cook until most of the juice has evaporated. Add the red wine. Combine the flour, thyme and cloves and when the wine has cooked down, sprinkle over the top and stir thoroughly, then add boiling stock or water. Put the meat back into the pan and simmer for 1 hour. Uncover and add the peas or artichoke hearts. Season with salt and pepper to taste.

Put a tablespoon or two of filling down the center of each crepe. Roll and turn seam side down in a buttered baking pan. Bake at 375° F. for 15 or 20 minutes. The crepes may be topped with tomato sauce if you like. This freezes well. Defrost completely and bake the same as freshly made.

CREPES WITH BEEF AND BEEF KIDNEY

1 pound stewing beef
¾ pound beef kidney
4 tablespoons drippings
   from beef fat
1 large onion,
   coarsely chopped
1 cup beef stock or
   bouillon

1 teaspoon Worcestershire
   sauce
1 tablespoon cornstarch
   mixed with
   1 tablespoon water
salt and pepper to taste
14–16 5-inch crepes

Cut the beef into small bite-size pieces. Trim the kidney, removing the center core. Heat the beef drippings in a large saucepan and brown the beef, kidney and onion over high heat. Add the stock and Worcestershire sauce and simmer covered for about 2 hours, adding more stock or bouillon if necessary. Mix the cornstarch with the water and add to the beef and kidney mixture, stirring until sauce is thick and clear. Season with salt and pepper to taste. Cool slightly.

Put a couple of spoonfuls of mixture down the center of each crepe. Roll and turn seam side down in a buttered baking pan. Bake for 20 minutes at 375° F. This freezes well. Defrost completely and bake the same as freshly made.

With Veal Fillings

CREPES WITH VEAL PAPRIKASH

1½ pounds boneless
   stewing veal
2 teaspoons paprika
2 onions, chopped
1 small clove garlic,
   minced
4 tablespoons butter

½ green pepper, chopped
1 tomato, chopped
1 cup chicken broth
¼ cup sour cream
salt and pepper to taste
14–16 5-inch crepes

Cut the veal into small pieces and sprinkle with the paprika. Let stand while sautéing chopped onions and minced garlic in butter in a heavy saucepan. Add veal and when it is seared on all sides, add chopped green pepper, tomato and chicken broth. Cover and simmer for about an hour or until fork tender. Remove from heat. Check seasoning, add salt and pepper to taste and more paprika if you like. Add sour cream and stir thoroughly.

Put a spoonful or two of filling down the center of each crepe. Roll and turn seam side down and place in a buttered baking dish. Bake for 20 minutes at 375° F. This freezes well. May be defrosted completely and baked the same as freshly made.

CREPES WITH VEAL AND CUCUMBERS

2 large cucumbers
1 pound veal for scallopini
3 tablespoons flour
3 tablespoons butter
3 tablespoons sherry or
   Marsala wine

½ cup heavy cream
salt and pepper to taste
14–16 5-inch crepes

Peel the cucumbers and cut them into sixths or eighths lengthwise and then into 2-inch pieces. Put in boiling salted water and cook just above a simmer for 7–8 minutes. Cucumbers should be fork tender but not falling to pieces. While the cucumbers are cooking, cut the veal into approximately 2-inch squares, dredge with the flour and cook over high heat in the sizzling butter in a large skillet. This is a very delicately flavored dish and unless the meat is well browned it won't have enough flavor. When the pieces are brown—2–3 minutes—add the sherry or Marsala and still over high heat let it almost evaporate. Add the cream and cook over medium heat until the sauce thickens.

By this time the cucumbers should be done. Drain them, let stand a minute or two so all the excess moisture is out and combine with the veal. Cook only a minute more. Cool slightly.

Put a couple of pieces of veal and a couple of pieces of cucumber down the middle of a plain crepe. Add a spoonful of the pan sauce, roll up and place seam side down in a buttered baking dish. Any sauce remaining in the pan should be spooned over the top of the crepes. Bake at 375° F. for 20 minutes. This does *not* freeze well.

CREPES WITH VEAL AND OLIVES

1½ pounds boneless
   stewing veal
2 tablespoons butter
2 tablespoons olive oil
1 cup chopped onions
1 clove garlic, chopped
¼ pound chopped ham
¾ cup pimiento olives

2 small tomatoes,
   finely chopped
½ cup white wine
½ to 1 cup chicken broth
   or veal stock
1 tablespoon cornstarch
salt and pepper to taste
14–16 5-inch crepes

Cut the veal into small pieces. Combine the butter and oil in a large skillet and when it is hot put in the veal and sear on all sides. Add the chopped onions and garlic and cook over medium-high heat until onions are limp. Add the chopped ham and cook for a minute or two more. Add the olives cut in half if small, in quarters if large, the tomatoes, the white wine and chicken broth. Transfer to a heavy-bottomed saucepan and simmer for about 40 minutes or until veal is tender. Add extra chicken broth if necessary. Mix the cornstarch with a little water and stir into the juices. Stir until sauce thickens. Taste for seasoning. If the olives and ham are salty, not much additional salt may be needed.

Put a spoonful or two of filling down the center of each crepe. Roll and place seam side down in a buttered baking dish. Bake at 400° F. for 15–20 minutes. This freezes well. Defrost completely and bake the same as freshly made.

VARIATION

CREPES WITH BEEF AND OLIVES
This is made the same as above, using stewing beef instead of veal and beef stock or bouillon instead of chicken broth or veal stock. Cooking time for the filling will be about an hour and a half.

CREPES WITH VEAL AND PROSCIUTTO

1 *pound of veal for scallopini*	2 *tablespoons parsley*
2 *tablespoons flour*	¼ *pound of prosciutto (Italian ham), chopped*
2 *tablespoons olive oil*	½ *teaspoon basil*
2 *tablespoons butter*	2 *fresh tomatoes, chopped*
1 *clove garlic, minced*	¼ *cup heavy cream*
2 *tablespoons chopped onion*	*salt and pepper to taste*
	14–16 5-inch crepes

Cut the thin veal slices into 1-inch squares. Dredge with flour. Heat the oil and butter and fry the veal over heat high enough to brown all sides. Set aside and in the same pan, sauté the minced garlic, chopped onion, parsley and chopped prosciutto. Add the basil and tomatoes. Cook over medium heat until the tomatoes are mushy. Break up with a fork, add ¼ cup heavy cream, salt and pepper to taste and cook until sauce thickens. Cool.

Put a spoonful or two of filling down the center of each crepe. Roll and place seam side down in a buttered baking dish. Bake at 375° F. for 20 minutes. This freezes well. Defrost completely and bake the same as freshly made.

CREPES WITH VEAL IN SOUR CREAM

1¼ pounds boneless
  stewing veal
1 onion, chopped
½ pound mushrooms,
  chopped
2 tablespoons butter

½ cup chicken broth
1 cup sour cream
1 teaspoon soy sauce
½ teaspoon dry mustard
salt and pepper to taste
14–16 5-inch crepes

Cut the veal into small pieces. Melt butter in a heavy pan and when it bubbles add the onion and sauté until limp. Add mushrooms and cook for another minute or two, then add the veal. When no color shows on the veal, add chicken broth and cook covered over low heat for about an hour, adding more broth if necessary. Combine the sour cream, soy sauce and mustard and mix into the veal over low heat. Add salt and pepper to taste.

Put a spoonful of filling down the center of each crepe. Roll and turn seam side down in a buttered baking dish. Bake for 20 minutes at 375° F. This does *not* freeze well.

CREPES WITH VEAL CACCIATORE

1 pound veal for scallopini   1 onion, chopped
2 tablespoons flour   2 cups canned tomatoes
2 tablespoons oil   salt and pepper to taste
2 tablespoons butter   14–16 5-inch crepes
1 green pepper, chopped
½ pound mushrooms,
   chopped

Cut the thin slices of veal into 1-inch squares. Dust with flour and brown in oil and butter for 2 or 3 minutes. Remove from pan and set aside. Sauté the green pepper, mushrooms and onion in the same pan until all the vegetables are limp. Add the canned tomatoes and cook until sauce begins to thicken. Return the veal to the pan and cook for another 2 or 3 minutes.

Put a spoonful or two of filling down the center of each crepe, roll and place seam side down in a buttered baking dish. Any sauce left in the pan can be brushed over top of crepes. Bake at 375° F. for 20 minutes. This freezes well. Defrost completely and bake the same as freshly made.

CREPES WITH VEAL PICCATA

1 *pound veal*	¼ *cup chicken broth*
2 *tablespoons flour*	(*if needed*)
1 *tablespoon butter*	*juice of one lemon*
1 *tablespoon oil*	*sprinkle grated lemon*
½ *pound mushrooms,*	*rind*
thinly sliced	*salt and pepper to taste*
¼ *cup white wine*	16 *5-inch crepes*

The best veal for this dish is veal cut and pounded for scallopini. In any case, the veal should be sliced thin and then cut into bite-size pieces. Dredge with the flour. Melt butter and oil in your largest skillet until bubbly and put in the pieces of veal and keep the heat high enough so that veal will brown on both sides but not burn. Add mushrooms to veal in skillet and cook for a minute or two. Then add white wine and let boil up. Simmer for a few minutes and if the sauce seems too thick, add a little chicken broth. Then add the juice of one lemon and just a sprinkle—a few gratings —of lemon peel. Season with salt and pepper to taste.

Butter a baking dish and fill 16 crepes with the cooled mixture. Use a spoonful or two for each crepe, roll up the crepes and turn seam side down. Heat in a 400° F. oven for 10 minutes. If a moister crepe is desired, pour a little chicken broth over the tops of the crepes. Because the sauce is not rich, this amount will serve 6 only if the rest of the meal is fairly substantial —2 vegetables and a salad; or a cream soup first or a rich dessert. May be frozen but should be thoroughly defrosted before baking the same as freshly made.

With Ham, Pork or Bacon Fillings

CREPES WITH HAM AND MUSHROOMS

1 *pound ham steak or smoked pork chops*
1 *pound mushrooms, coarsely chopped*
4 *tablespoons butter*
2 *tablespoons Madeira wine*
2 *tablespoons flour*
1½ *cups brown stock or bouillon*
salt and pepper to taste
14–16 *5-inch crepes, either plain or made with beef bouillon*

Cut ham or pork into small cubes, less than half an inch square. Melt butter in large skillet and when it bubbles up add the mushrooms. Stir and turn over until mushrooms are well coated with butter, then add ham or pork cubes. Cook for 2 or 3 minutes, then add Madeira. Mix flour with a small amount of the bouillon. Add to the pan with the rest of the bouillon and cook and stir for 10 minutes over low heat until sauce is thickened. Test for seasoning.

Put a spoonful or two of the ham mixture down the center of each crepe. Roll and turn seam side down in a buttered baking dish. Spread any leftover sauce over the tops of the crepes, or if you wish, pour a cup of brown sauce over the crepes. Bake at 375° F. for 20 minutes. This freezes well. Defrost completely and bake the same as freshly made.

CREPES WITH HAM AND HAZELNUTS

2 tablespoons butter
¼ pound mushrooms,
    coarsely chopped
1 tablespoon minced
    onion
1½ cups ham,
    coarsely chopped
1 cup hazelnuts,
    coarsely chopped
½ cup peas, spinach
    or asparagus

½ cup chicken broth
¼ cup cream
2 teaspoons cornstarch
salt and pepper to taste
14–16 5-inch crepes
Optional Topping:
whipped cream
grated cheese
chopped hazelnuts

Heat butter in a large skillet until it bubbles. Put in the mushrooms and the minced onion and sauté over medium heat for 2 or 3 minutes. Add the ham and hazelnuts and cook only until they are coated with the butter. Add green vegetables (if asparagus, cut into half-inch pieces) and add chicken broth. Stir the cornstarch into the cream and stir into the mixture, cooking until sauce thickens. Check the seasonings.

Put a spoonful or two of the filling down the center of each crepe. Roll and turn seam side down in a buttered baking dish. If you wish, a little heavy cream salted and whipped may be spread over the top of the crepes and sprinkled with grated cheese and chopped hazelnuts. Bake at 375° F. for 20 minutes. This freezes well, either with or without the topping. Topping may be put over the defrosted crepes and they may be baked the same as freshly made. Or in a freezer-to-oven pan, bake at 300° F. for 40 minutes and then 375° F. for 15 minutes.

CREPES WITH DEVILED HAM

2 cups chopped or
  ground ham
1 tablespoon minced
  green pepper
1 cup sour cream

2 teaspoons prepared
  mustard
¼ teaspoon cayenne
½ teaspoon black pepper
12–14 5-inch crepes

The ham should be finely chopped or ground with the finest blade of a meat grinder. Add the green pepper. Mix the sour cream with the mustard, cayenne and black pepper and stir it into the ham and green pepper. For a smoother filling the mixture may be put in the blender for a minute.

Butter a baking pan and put two spoonfuls of the mixture down the center of each crepe. Roll and turn seam side down. Spread a little butter over the tops of the crepes and bake at 375° F. for 15 or 20 minutes. This freezes well but is best if defrosted completely and then baked the same as freshly made.

CREPES WITH CHINESE MEATBALLS

¾ pound ground pork
¼ pound ground beef
1 tablespoon butter
¼ pound mushrooms,
   finely chopped
1 tablespoon finely
   chopped onion
½ cup chopped water
   chestnuts

1 tablespoon soy sauce
½ teaspoon nutmeg
1 egg
salt and pepper to taste
1½ cups brown stock
   or bouillon
1 tablespoon cornstarch
2 tablespoons sherry
14–16 5-inch crepes

Mix the meats in a bowl. Melt 1 tablespoon of butter in a large skillet and add the chopped mushrooms and onion. Cook until limp. Add the chopped water chestnuts, soy sauce and nutmeg to the mixed meats. Beat the egg with a fork and mix it into the meat mixture. To test for seasoning, sauté a tiny amount of the mixture. Be sure to cook thoroughly because it contains pork. Add salt and pepper and more soy sauce if needed.

Form into tiny balls and sauté until brown on all sides and well cooked. Shake the pan occasionally as the meatballs are cooking. Remove the meatballs and add bouillon to the pan, scraping up all the browned particles. Mix the cornstarch with the sherry and add to the boiling juices in the pan. Cook until clear and well thickened.

Butter a baking dish and put 4 or 5 meatballs and a spoonful of sauce on each crepe. Roll and turn seam side down in a buttered baking dish. If there is sauce left, spread it over the top of the crepes. Bake at

375° F. for 20 minutes. These may be frozen and baked the same as freshly made after defrosting. Or in a freezer-to-oven pan they may be baked before defrosting for 40 minutes at 300° F. and 15 minutes at 375° F.

CREPES WITH SWEET AND SOUR PORK

1 tablespoon soy sauce	⅔ cup pineapple juice
2 tablespoons sherry	1 tablespoon soy sauce
4 tablespoons cornstarch	1 tablespoon cornstarch
1½ pounds lean pork, cut in ½-inch cubes	1 green pepper
	½ cup carrots
peanut oil	2 tablespoons peanut oil
½ cup sugar	1 cup pineapple chunks
2 tablespoons catsup	1 clove garlic, minced
¼ cup vinegar	14–16 5-inch crepes

Mix soy sauce, sherry and cornstarch and stir into the pork cubes so that all are coated. Let stand about a half hour, turning occasionally. Put enough peanut oil in a heavy pan so that it will just cover the pork cubes. Heat the oil until it is bubbling and put in only as many cubes of the coated pork as will fit without crowding. Cook about 6 or 7 minutes turning so that pork cubes are browned on all sides. Remove from pan. Cook remaining cubes and set aside.

For the sweet and sour sauce combine sugar, catsup, vinegar, pineapple juice (add water if necessary to make ⅔ cup) soy sauce and cornstarch first mixed with part of the liquid. Cook until it comes to a boil and becomes thick and clear. Cut the green pepper and the carrots in uneven but fairly small slices—not much bigger than the pork. Heat 2 tablespoons of peanut oil in a large skillet, add the green pepper, carrots and garlic and stir and fry over high heat. Add the pineapple chunks and continue stirring, then add fried pork and finally the sweet and sour sauce. Cook for another 5 minutes. Put a couple of spoonfuls of mixture down the center of each crepe. Roll and place seam side down in a buttered pan. Brush the tops with the sauce that remains in the pan. Bake at 375° F. for about 20 minutes. Does *not* freeze well.

CREPES WITH CHINESE PORK, WATER CHESTNUTS AND SNOW PEAS

1 *pound of lean uncooked pork cut in paper-thin slices*	3 *tablespoons peanut oil*
	1 *package frozen snow peas, partially defrosted*
2 *scallions, shredded*	1 *small can water chestnuts, sliced*
1 *tablespoon soy sauce*	
1 *tablespoon sherry*	½ *cup chicken broth*
2 *teaspoons cornstarch*	2 *teaspoons cornstarch*
2 *or 3 slices fresh ginger root (optional)*	*salt if needed*
	14–16 *5-inch crepes*

The pork must be cut into very thin slices so it will cook through. Thin slicing is facilitated by partially freezing the meat before slicing. Put it into a bowl with the shredded scallions, soy sauce, sherry, cornstarch and finely cut up ginger root. Let stand half an hour. Heat 2 tablespoons peanut oil in a large skillet. Separate the partially defrosted snow peas and turn into the heated oil in the skillet. Cook and stir over high heat for 2 or 3 minutes. Turn into a bowl.

Put the third tablespoon of oil into the pan and heat

until bubbling. Turn the marinated pork slices into the pan and cook and stir over high heat for 3 or 4 minutes. Return the snow peas to the pan, add the sliced water chestnuts. Mix 1 tablespoon of the chicken broth with the 2 teaspoons of cornstarch. Pour the rest into the skillet with the pork and vegetables. When the liquid begins to boil, stir in the cornstarch and continue cooking until the sauce thickens and is clear.

Put a spoonful or two of the mixture down the center of each crepe. Roll and turn seam side down in a buttered baking dish. Brush the tops of the crepes with the remaining liquid. Bake at 375° F. for 15 or 20 minutes. This does *not* freeze well.

CREPES WITH BACON, GREEN ONIONS AND CHEESE

1 *pound thinly sliced bacon*
4 *or 5 bunches of green onions (with tops)*
2 *tablespoons butter*

½ *pound sharp American or cheddar cheese, shredded*
12 *5-inch crepes*

Fry the bacon until brown and crisp. Drain on paper towels and crumble. Clean the onions, retaining as much of the green tops as are firm and fresh. Slice into diagonal shreds or cut lengthwise into quarters and then into 2-inch pieces. Pour off the fat from frying the bacon, leaving only what clings to the pan, and add the butter. Heat until butter is bubbling, add the green onions and cook for 3 or 4 minutes until onions are limp.

Butter a baking dish. Put a spoonful of green onions

along the center of each crepe, then a spoonful of crumbled bacon, then a spoonful of shredded cheese. Save enough cheese to spread on top of rolled crepes. Roll each crepe, turn seam side down in a buttered baking dish and sprinkle remaining cheese on top. Bake for 15 minutes on the top shelf of a 400-450° F. oven. This freezes well. Defrost completely and bake the same as freshly made.

With Lamb Fillings

CREPES WITH LAMB IN ORANGE SAUCE

2½ cups of leftover roast
  lamb
1 onion, chopped
1 garlic clove, chopped
2 tablespoons butter
½ cup red wine
½ cup lamb or beef stock
  or lamb gravy
1 teaspoon grated orange
  rind

1 teaspoon powdered
  mint
2 tablespoons chopped
  parsley
1 tomato, peeled and
  chopped
¼ cup milk
1 slice white bread
salt and pepper to taste
14–16 5-inch crepes

Cut lamb into small pieces. Sauté onion and garlic clove in butter. Add lamb, red wine and stock, grated orange rind, mint and parsley. Simmer over low heat and add chopped tomato. Crumble bread into milk and add to lamb. Season to taste. Cook over medium heat until well thickened.

Cool slightly and put a spoonful or two of lamb mixture down the center of each crepe. Roll and turn seam side down on a buttered baking dish. Bake for 20 minutes at 375° F. This does *not* freeze well.

CREPES WITH LEMON LAMB

1½ pounds of boneless
    lamb
2 tablespoons butter
3 scallions, chopped
1 teaspoon dried dill weed
1 teaspoon crushed mint
    leaves
1 tablespoon chopped
    parsley

¼ cup white wine
½ cup stock or water
salt and pepper to taste
2 teaspoons cornstarch
1 tablespoon water
juice of one lemon
1 egg and 1 egg yolk
14–16 5-inch crepes

Cut the lamb into small pieces. Heat the butter in a heavy pan until bubbling and add the lamb and scallions, cooking over low heat until scallions are wilted and lamb is seared. Add dill weed, mint leaves, parsley, the white wine and the stock or water. Taste for seasoning. Simmer for about an hour or until lamb is tender. Mix the cornstarch and water and stir into the stew off the heat. Add the lemon juice and return to low heat, stirring until thickened. Beat the egg and the egg yolk until thick, add a little of the hot sauce gradually to the eggs and then add to the lamb mixture.

Spread a spoonful or two of mixture down the center of each crepe. Roll and turn seam side down in a buttered baking dish. Bake at 375° F. for 20 minutes. This does *not* freeze well.

CREPES MOUSSAKA

1 eggplant, peeled and diced	2 tablespoons chopped parsley
4 tablespoons butter	¼ teaspoon cinnamon
1 onion, finely chopped	¼ cup grated Parmesan cheese
1 pound ground lamb	
¼ cup red wine	salt and pepper to taste
1 tomato, peeled and chopped	14–16 5-inch crepes

Custard Topping:

2 tablespoons butter	2 eggs
2 tablespoons flour	½ teaspoon nutmeg
2 cups milk or half milk and half cream	1 cup grated Parmesan cheese

Sauté diced eggplant quickly in 2 tablespoons of butter and set aside. Chop the onion and sauté in the rest of the butter. Add the ground lamb and brown lightly, stirring with a fork so that the meat is well crumbled. Add red wine, peeled tomato, parsley and cinnamon and cook for about 20 minutes until the moisture is absorbed. Add the grated cheese, mix well and remove from heat. Add salt and pepper to taste. Mix in the eggplant and cool slightly.

For the custard topping, melt the butter, add the flour and cook, stirring until well blended but not at all browned. Meanwhile, heat the milk or part milk and cream. Remove the butter and flour from the heat and add the hot milk and stir until slightly thickened. Beat the eggs only until frothy and stir into the sauce off heat. Add the nutmeg and half the grated cheese.

Put a tablespoon or two of the filling down the center of each crepe, roll and place seam side down in a baking dish at least 1½ inches high. Pour the topping over crepes and sprinkle the rest of the cheese over the sauce. Bake at 375° F. for 30–40 minutes. This will take longer than most sauces to set. This freezes well; defrost completely and bake the same as freshly made.

CREPES WITH CURRIED LAMB I

2 pounds boneless lamb
3 tablespoons butter
1 cup sliced onions
2 cloves garlic, peeled
  and left whole
1½ cups milk
1 slice fresh ginger root or
  ½ teaspoon powdered
  ginger
2 teaspoons curry powder

½ teaspoon salt
½ teaspoon black pepper
2 tablespoons lemon juice
grated rind of 1 lemon
½ cup cream
2 teaspoons cornstarch
butter
14–16 5-inch crepes
½ cup grated almonds or
  cashew nuts

Remove fat from lamb and cut into bite-size pieces. Brown in butter and add onions and garlic. Sauté over low heat for half an hour, remove garlic and add milk, ginger root cut in tiny dice or powdered ginger, curry powder, salt, pepper, lemon juice and grated rind and cook for another 10 minutes. Mix cream with cornstarch and add to pan, stirring until thickened. Cool.

Butter a baking pan. Put a teaspoonful or two of the curried lamb down the center of a crepe, roll and turn seam side down. Brush with butter and sprinkle with grated nuts. Bake in a 400° F. oven for 15 minutes. This freezes well; defrost and bake the same as freshly made. In a freezer-to-oven pan bake at 300° F. for 40 minutes then at 400° F. for 15 minutes.

CREPES WITH CURRIED LAMB II

2 pounds lean uncooked lamb or leftover roast lamb
½ cup sliced onions
4 tablespoons butter
1 tablespoon curry powder
3 tablespoons flour
2 cups stock or water
2 medium apples, peeled and cut in small pieces

2 teaspoons grated lime peel
1 cup slivered toasted almonds
salt and pepper to taste
14–16 5-inch crepes
½ cup grated almonds for topping

Cut lamb into small pieces. Sauté onions in butter in a large skillet for 5 minutes until limp but not brown. Add lamb and stir to coat with butter. Sprinkle curry powder and flour over lamb and onions and mix well. If lamb is raw, cook for 20 or 30 minutes, then add stock or water and cut-up apples. Sauté for another 10 minutes, stirring occasionally, add grated lime peel and slivered toasted almonds and cool slightly. Check seasonings.

Put a spoonful or two down the center of each crepe, roll and turn seam side down in a buttered baking dish. Sprinkle the tops with grated almonds and bake for 20 minutes in a 375° F. oven. This freezes well. Defrost completely and bake the same as freshly made.

With Chicken or Turkey Fillings

CREPES WITH CHICKEN GIBLETS OR HEARTS

2 pounds chicken giblets
   or hearts
1 stalk celery
1 carrot
1 onion
1 teaspoon salt
2 chopped onions
½ pound chopped
   mushrooms
3 tablespoons butter

2 teaspoons soy sauce
2 tomatoes, finely diced
2 cups chicken broth
   from giblets
2 tablespoons cornstarch
   dissolved in a little
   water
salt and pepper to taste
14–16 5-inch crepes

Cover cleaned giblets or hearts with water. Add celery, carrot and onion each cut in four pieces and 1 teaspoon salt. Bring to a boil. Skin and simmer until tender— about one hour. Trim gristle off giblets and cut into pieces. Cut hearts in half. Save broth and add chicken broth, fresh or canned, to make 2 cups.

Heat butter in a large skillet to bubbling, add onions and brown slightly. Add mushrooms and cook for about 5 minutes more. Add soy sauce and tomatoes. (It is not necessary to peel them.) Cook until tomatoes are mushy, then add chicken broth and cook for another 5 minutes. Dissolve cornstarch in water and stir into the mixture. Cook for 3 or 4 minutes until sauce thickens. Cool slightly.

Put a spoonful or two of mixture down the center of each crepe. Roll and turn seam side down in a buttered baking dish. Remaining sauce in pan can be brushed over tops of crepes. Bake at 375° F. for 20 minutes. This freezes well. Defrost completely and bake the same as freshly made.

CREPES WITH CHICKEN SPANISH STYLE

1 medium-sized broiling chicken or 1½ cups leftover cooked turkey or chicken

1 cup chopped onion

¼ pound mushrooms, chopped

1 small green pepper, chopped

4 tablespoons fat (half butter, half oil)

2 tomatoes, peeled and chopped, or 1 cup canned

2 cut up chorizos (Spanish sausage) or 2 hot Italian sausages

1 cup red wine

1 pound fresh peas, shelled, or ½ package frozen peas

1 cup chicken or turkey broth

salt and pepper to taste

18–20 5-inch crepes

tomato sauce for topping (optional)

Cook chicken as directed in recipe on page 87 or use leftover turkey or chicken. Cut chicken into bite-size pieces.

Chop onions, mushrooms and green pepper fairly fine. Melt butter and add oil in large skillet or stewing pan. When it is bubbly add onion and lower heat so that onion does not brown but becomes limp and golden. When fat is clear again, add mushrooms and green pepper to pan. Cook for 2 or 3 minutes, then add tomatoes and chorizos. Cook for another 5 to 10 minutes until mixture begins to thicken, then add red wine and peas. Cook for another 5 minutes and add broth. Add chicken and season to taste. Simmer for another few minutes until sauce thickens again. Cool.

Butter a baking dish and fill crepes generously using 2 or 3 spoonfuls. Roll up the crepes and turn seam side down. These may be covered with tomato sauce or left plain. Bake in a 400° F. oven 10 to 15 minutes. They may be frozen, with or without sauce. Allow to defrost for at least 2 hours and bake the same as freshly made. Or in a freezer-to-oven pan, bake in a 300° F. oven for 40 minutes then raise to 400° F. and bake 10 minutes more.

CREPES WITH CHICKEN PAPRIKASH

1 medium frying chicken or 2 cups leftover turkey or chicken
4 tablespoons butter
1½ cups coarsely chopped onions
1 large green pepper, cored, seeded and finely chopped
½ cup chopped celery
1 cup tomato juice
4 teaspoons (or more) Hungarian sweet paprika
½ cup sour cream
salt and pepper to taste
14–16 5-inch crepes

Stew chicken as in recipe on page 87 or measure 2 cups leftover turkey or chicken.

Melt butter in large skillet and when it bubbles up add onions. Sauté until golden and limp and butter is clear. Add chopped green pepper and celery and cook about 2 minutes. Then add ½ cup tomato juice, cover and cook for about 5 minutes more. Sprinkle paprika over chicken or turkey and add to the vegetables. Add more of the tomato juice if needed and simmer for 3 or 4 minutes. Add sour cream and cook over low heat just a minute or two more. Season with salt and pepper to taste.

Butter a baking pan, put a spoonful or two of filling in each crepe, roll up and turn seam side down. Bake in a 400° F. oven for 10–15 minutes. May be baked plain or cover with sour cream sprinkled with more paprika. May be frozen in a freezer-to-oven pan, baked at 300° F. 40 minutes, then at 400° F. for 15 minutes.

CREPES WITH CHICKEN, WALNUTS AND HAM

uncooked breasts from   *¼ pound diced ham*
  2 chickens   *1 cup grated walnuts*
1 teaspoon soy sauce   *1 cup chicken broth*
2 tablespoons sherry   *2 teaspoons cornstarch*
1 teaspoon cornstarch   *14–16 5-inch crepes*
1 tablespoon peanut oil

Cut the raw chicken breasts into small pieces. Mix together the soy sauce, sherry and 1 teaspoon cornstarch and pour over the cut-up chicken. Let stand half an hour. Heat the peanut oil in a large skillet over medium-high heat. Put the marinated chicken into the pan and stir rapidly over high heat until the chicken becomes opaque and white—about 3 or 4 minutes. Add the diced ham and the walnuts, cook over moderate heat a minute or so, then add all but a tablespoon of the chicken broth. Dissolve the cornstarch in the remaining tablespoon of broth, stir it into the mixture and cook over low heat for two or three minutes.

Butter a baking pan. Put a tablespoon or two of filling on each crepe, roll and turn seam side down. If you wish, the tops can be sprinkled with more grated walnuts, moistened with a little extra chicken broth or spread with softened butter. Bake in a 375° F. oven for 15 minutes. These may be frozen and are best if completely defrosted and baked the same as freshly made.

CREPES WITH CHICKEN AND TANGERINES

2 frying chickens
½ teaspoon salt
1 stalk celery
1 teaspoon dried parsley
1 carrot
2 tablespoons flour
4 tablespoons butter
½ cup white wine
2 tablespoons Cointreau
½ pound sliced mushrooms
2 tangerines cut in sections
½ cup heavy cream
½ cup chopped almonds
16 5-inch crepes

Disjoint chicken. Bone out breast and thigh meat and set aside. Put bones and rest of chicken in a small saucepan with salt, celery, parsley and carrot and water to cover. Simmer for 40 minutes to an hour. Drain broth and reduce to one cup.

Cut chicken breasts and thighs into small pieces, dust with flour and sauté in half the butter. Add the cup of chicken broth and the white wine and the Cointreau and simmer for 15 minutes. Sauté mushrooms in the rest of the butter and add to chicken mixture. Slit seed side of tangerine sections and remove seeds.

Add tangerine sections with heavy cream and continue cooking until sauce thickens. Cool slightly.

Butter a baking pan. Put a spoonful of filling along center of each crepe, roll and turn seam side down. Sprinkle tops with chopped almonds. Bake in 375° F. oven for 15 to 20 minutes. These freeze well and may be defrosted and baked the same as freshly made. Or if in a freezer-to-oven pan, bake without defrosting at 300° F. for 30 minutes and 375° F. for 15 minutes.

CREPES WITH CHICKEN EMPANADA STYLE

1 chicken, about 2½ pounds	grated rind of 1 lemon
1 small onion	nutmeg
1 stalk celery	black pepper
1 teaspoon salt	parsley
4 egg yolks	18 5-inch crepes
2 tablespoons lemon juice	

Disjoint chicken. Put in saucepan with onion cut in half, celery and salt. Add water barely to cover, bring to a boil, then simmer for about 30 minutes or until chicken is tender. Remove meat from bones and return bones to saucepan and simmer 30 minutes longer. Strain broth and return to saucepan. Boil quickly and reduce broth to one cup.

Beat egg yolks with lemon juice and rind and pour hot broth into the egg and lemon mixture, beating well. Return to pan and cook over low heat until sauce thickens. Stir in a sprinkle of nutmeg and black pepper and some chopped parsley. Chop chicken into small pieces and pour sauce over it in bowl. Mix well and chill for several hours.

Put a spoonful or two of the mixture on each crepe, roll and turn seam side down on a buttered baking dish. Sprinkle with a little chicken broth and lemon juice or melted butter and bake at 375° F. for 20 minutes. These freeze well. They are best if completely defrosted and baked the same as freshly made.

CREPES FILLED WITH TURKEY DIVAN SUPREME

18 thin slices of leftover turkey breast
18 paper-thin slices of prosciutto (Italian ham)
18 thin slices of Swiss cheese
18 pieces of broccoli
18 5-inch crepes
2 cups Mornay sauce (page 174)
grated Parmesan, Swiss or sharp white cheddar

The turkey slices should be about 5 inches by 3 or 4 inches and the prosciutto and Swiss cheese should be the same size or smaller. Wash and strip broccoli so that stalks measure no more than 5 inches. Cut each stalk into 3 or 4 pieces lengthwise depending on size. Cook in a large quantity of boiling water until barely tender (about 10 minutes). Drain into colander and run cold water over broccoli.

Butter a flat baking dish and place on each crepe one slice of turkey, then one slice of prosciutto, one slice of cheese and one piece of broccoli. Spoon a little Mornay sauce over the broccoli, roll up crepe and turn seam side down in the baking dish. Top the filled crepes with the remaining Mornay sauce and sprinkle grated cheese over the top. Bake in a 400° F. oven for 15 minutes. If not browned on top slip under the broiler for a minute or two. Serve with a mixed green salad or lettuce and grapefruit. This does *not* freeze well.

CREPES WITH CURRIED CHICKEN

2 cups cooked chicken, cut in small cubes
4 tablespoons butter
1 medium onion, chopped
1 stalk celery, finely diced
1 teaspoon chopped parsley
1 tablespoon curry powder (or to taste)
1 tomato, chopped
salt and pepper to taste
1 cup chicken broth
1 tablespoon cornstarch
½ cup cream
½ cup ground cashew nuts
14–16 5-inch crepes
chopped cashew nuts for topping

Heat butter in large skillet, sauté onion and celery for 3 or 4 minutes, add parsley, curry powder and tomato. Check seasonings and add salt and pepper to taste. Cover and cook for 10 minutes. Add chicken broth, reserving 1 tablespoon to blend with the cornstarch. When the mixture returns to a boil, stir in the cornstarch, lower heat and stir until well thickened. Add cut-up chicken and cream and cook about 5 minutes until sauce is thickened again. Stir in ground cashew nuts and remove from heat.

Put a spoonful or two of filling down the center of each crepe, roll and turn seam side down in a buttered baking dish. Any sauce left in the pan can be spread over tops of the crepes with the chopped cashew nuts.

Bake at 375° F. for 20 minutes. This freezes well; just defrost completely and bake the same as freshly made.

CREPES WITH CHICKEN HASH

2 cups chopped cooked
   chicken or turkey
1 tablespoon chopped
   fresh parsley
1 teaspoon grated onion
½ cup cream
1 egg yolk

2 cups medium cream
   sauce (page 172)
3 strips of bacon cooked,
   drained and crumbled
½ cup Swiss and Parmesan
   cheese grated together
14–16 5-inch crepes

Simmer the cooked chicken, parsley and grated onion in a half cup of cream for about 5 minutes. Combine the egg yolk with half of the cream sauce and add to the chicken mixture. Cook for a few minutes until sauce is thick and add the crumbled bacon and half of the grated cheese.

Spread a spoonful or two of the chicken hash on each crepe, roll and turn seam side down in a buttered baking dish. Pour the other cup of cream sauce (or more if you like) over the top of the crepes and sprinkle the rest of the grated cheese. Bake for 15 minutes at 375° F. This freezes well; defrost completely and bake the same as freshly made.

CREPES WITH CHILI CHICKEN

2 cups cooked chicken
   (or turkey)
4 tablespoons butter
1 onion, chopped
1 green pepper, seeded
   and chopped
½ cup chopped black
   olives
1 cup canned or fresh cut
   up tomatoes

½ teaspoon oregano
1 tablespoon chili powder
   (or to taste)
¼ cup grated sharp
   cheddar or Parmesan
   cheese
salt and pepper to taste
14–16 5-inch crepes
½ cup grated cheese
   for topping

Cut chicken into small pieces. Heat butter in large skillet until it bubbles, add the onion and green pepper and cook until they are limp but not brown. Add the chicken and stir to coat it with the butter. Add the black olives and the tomatoes, the oregano and the chili powder and cook 15 minutes, or until much of the juice has evaporated.

Put a spoonful or two of the mixture down the center of each crepe, roll and turn seam side down in a buttered baking dish. Put a spoonful of the grated cheese over the top of each crepe. Bake at 375° F. for 15 minutes. This freezes well. Defrost completely and then bake the same as freshly made.

CREPES WITH CHICKEN MARENGO

1 2½-pound chicken
4 tablespoons butter
¼ pound small mush-
    rooms, quartered
2 tomatoes, peeled and
    chopped
½ cup white wine
16 cooked and peeled
    shrimp, sliced in half
    lengthwise

1 clove garlic, finely
    chopped
½ cup chicken broth
2 teaspoons cornstarch
salt and pepper to taste
2 sliced hard-boiled eggs
14–16 5-inch crepes

Remove the chicken meat from the bones and cut it in small pieces. Heat butter until it is bubbling, and brown the pieces of chicken in it. When the chicken is brown, add the mushrooms and brown lightly. Add the tomatoes and cook for 2 or 3 minutes before adding the white wine. Cook over a medium-high flame until the juices are cut down by half, add the shrimp, garlic and most of the chicken broth. Dissolve the cornstarch in the rest of the broth and add it to the pan, stirring until thickened. Check seasoning and add the sliced hard-boiled eggs. Cool slightly.

Spread a spoonful or two of the filling down the center of each crepe. Roll and place seam side down in a buttered baking dish. Bake at 375° F. for 15–20 minutes. This freezes well. Defrost completely and bake the same as freshly made.

This is an adaptation of the famous dish served to Napoleon after the Battle of Marengo from food "liberated" from the countryside. The original dish was supposed to include chicken, mushrooms, tomatoes, white wine and garlic. Instead of shrimp, crayfish were used and instead of hard-boiled eggs, fried eggs as a garnish.

CREPES WITH CHICKEN AND SNOW PEAS

1 3-pound chicken or 2 whole chicken breasts (uncooked)
2 scallions
2 tablespoons dry sherry
2 teaspoons cornstarch
1 teaspoon soy sauce
1 package frozen snow peas (edible pea pods)

1 can bamboo shoots
4 tablespoons peanut oil
¼ pound mushrooms, sliced
½ cup chicken broth
1 teaspoon cornstarch
½ cup toasted almonds
14–16 5-inch crepes

Skin and bone the chicken or chicken breasts and cut the meat into small pieces. Shred 2 scallions, mix with sherry, cornstarch and soy sauce and stir the chicken pieces into the mixture, turning over and over to get all pieces coated. Let stand for 20 minutes.

Partially defrost snow peas so that they are thawed enough to break apart. Cut the bamboo shoots into small pieces. Heat 2 tablespoons of the peanut oil in a large skillet, put in the snow peas and stir until they are coated with oil, add the bamboo shoots and mushrooms and stir and cook over high heat for 3 minutes. Turn into a warm dish.

Heat the rest of the peanut oil and stir—fry the cut-up chicken over high heat for 3 or 4 minutes. Add the chicken broth and the vegetables that have been set aside. Mix 1 teaspoon of cornstarch with a little water and add to the pan liquid, stirring until thick. Add toasted almonds. Cool slightly.

Put a spoonful or two of the filling down the center of each crepe. Roll and turn seam side down and place in a buttered baking dish. Brush what is left of the pan juices over the top and bake at 375° F. for 15 minutes. This does *not* freeze well, but may be made several hours in advance.

CREPES WITH CHICKEN AND SWEETBREADS

1 small frying chicken or 2 cups cooked turkey	½ pound mushrooms, chopped
1 stalk celery	¼ cup white wine
1 scraped carrot	2 egg yolks
1 small onion	½ cup heavy cream
parsley	salt and pepper to taste
salt	14–16 crepes
1 pair sweetbreads	2 to 3 cups medium cream
juice of 1 lemon	sauce (page 172)
1 medium onion, chopped	grated cheese or
2 tablespoons butter	breadcrumbs

Simmer the chicken in water just to cover with celery, carrot, onion, parsley and salt. Cut it into cubes or cut leftover turkey into cubes. Simmer the sweetbreads for 20 minutes in salted water to which the juice of a lemon has been added. Cool immediately in cold water, remove the connective tissue and tubes and slice.

Sauté the chopped onion in the butter. Add the mushrooms and sauté until limp. Add the cubed chicken, sliced sweetbreads and wine and cook over medium heat until the wine is mostly absorbed. Combine the egg yolks and cream and beat with a fork. Add to the chicken and sweetbread mixture and stir over low heat until the sauce thickens.

Butter a baking dish. Put two generous spoonfuls of mixture down the center of each crepe, roll and turn seam side down. Pour cream sauce over the top, sprinkle lightly with grated cheese or breadcrumbs and bake at 400° F. for 15 minutes. This freezes well and may be frozen with the cream sauce. Or add the cream sauce after filled crepes are defrosted, then bake the same as freshly made.

CREPES WITH CHICKEN AND MUSHROOMS

2½ cups cooked chicken
 or turkey
4 tablespoons butter
1 onion, chopped
1 pound mushrooms,
 chopped

2 tablespoons sherry
3 cups Mornay sauce
salt and pepper to taste
14–16 5-inch crepes
½ cup grated cheese
 for topping

Cut the chicken or turkey into bite-size pieces. Heat butter in large skillet and sauté onion until clear. Add mushrooms and cook for 2 or 3 minutes, then add chicken or turkey and sherry and stir to combine with butter and juices. Add one cup of Mornay sauce and stir and cook over low heat until sauce thickens. Cool slightly.

Put a spoonful or two of filling down the center of each crepe. Roll and turn seam side down and place in a buttered baking dish. Pour the other two cups of Mornay sauce over the filled crepes and sprinkle with grated cheese. Bake for 15 minutes at 375° F. This freezes well. Defrost completely then bake the same as freshly made.

CREPES WITH CHICKEN, HAM AND MUSHROOMS

2 cups cooked chicken
  or turkey
1 cup ham cut in bite-size
  pieces
4 tablespoons butter
1 onion, chopped
½ pound mushrooms,
  chopped

2 tablespoons Madeira
3 cups medium cream
  sauce
14–16 5-inch crepes
½ cup grated cheese
  for topping

Cut up chicken and ham and set aside. Heat the butter in a large skillet until it bubbles and sauté the onion until clear but not brown. Add the mushrooms and sauté for 2 or 3 minutes, then add the chicken and ham and the Madeira. Add one cup of sauce to chicken and ham mixture, cook until sauce thickens.

Put a spoonful or two of filling down the center of each crepe. Roll and turn seam side down in a buttered baking dish. Pour rest of cream sauce over crepes and sprinkle with grated cheese. Bake at 375° F. degrees for 20 minutes. This freezes well. Defrost completely and bake the same as freshly made.

CREPES WITH CHICKEN FLORENTINE

2 cups cooked chicken
  or turkey
4 tablespoons butter
2 onions, chopped
¼ pound mushrooms,
  chopped
1 package frozen
  chopped spinach

1 cup grated Parmesan
  or Swiss cheese
salt and pepper to taste
3 cups medium cream
  sauce
14–16 5-inch crepes

Cut chicken or turkey into small pieces. Heat butter in a large skillet until bubbling. Cook onions until they are clear, add mushrooms and cook until limp. Add chicken and stir to combine with the pan juices. Cook frozen spinach and drain thoroughly. Add to chicken mixture with a half cup of the cheese. Add a cup of cream sauce and mix well.

Put a spoonful or two of filling down the center of each crepe. Roll and turn seam side down in a buttered baking dish. Use 2 cups of cream sauce and remaining cheese for topping. Bake at 375° F. for 20 minutes. This freezes well. Defrost and bake the same as freshly made.

With Fish and Seafood Fillings

CREPES DELICES DE MER

3 cups cooked lobster, crabmeat, scallops and shrimps
4 tablespoons butter
2 tablespoons finely chopped shallots or onions
½ pound mushrooms, sliced

3 cups Mornay sauce (page 174)
salt and pepper to taste
16–18 5-inch crepes
½ cup grated Parmesan cheese
½ cup whipped cream (optional)

Use fresh, canned or frozen lobster, shrimp and crabmeat and fresh sea or bay scallops, if available. Any one of the various shellfish can be omitted. But a little lobster adds color and its special flavor to the dish.

Heat butter to bubbling and sauté shallots or onions and sliced mushrooms until quite limp but not brown. Add salt and pepper to taste and one cup of Mornay sauce.

Put a spoonful or two of filling down center of each crepe. Roll and place seam side down in a buttered baking dish. Top with the other 2 cups of Mornay sauce and sprinkle cheese over the top. Bake at 375° F. for 20 minutes. This freezes well. Omit the cheese before freezing and sprinkle over the top just before baking. Or spread one-half cup of whipped cream mixed with the cheese over the top of frozen crepes before baking.

Frozen crepes should be completely defrosted and then baked the same as freshly made.

CREPES WITH DEVILED CRAB

1 pound crabmeat (fresh, frozen or canned)
¾ cup chopped onions
2 stalks celery, chopped
8 tablespoons butter
1 cup rich cream sauce (page 173)

½ teaspoon Worcestershire sauce
½ teaspoon dry mustard
salt and pepper to taste
½ cup chopped black olives
14–16 5-inch crepes

Pick over fresh or canned crabmeat and flake. Or defrost frozen crabmeat. Heat butter to bubbling in a large skillet and sauté onions and celery until wilted and free of moisture. Add crabmeat and stir to combine with the butter. To a cup of rich cream sauce add Worcestershire sauce and dry mustard, salt and pepper to taste. If a hotter flavor is preferred, add more seasoning or a speck of cayenne. Stir sauce into crabmeat along with black olives and cook only until thickened.

Put a spoonful or two of filling down the center of each crepe, roll and turn seam side down in a buttered baking dish. If you wish, more cream sauce or buttered crumbs may be spread over tops of the crepes. Bake at 375° F. for 20 minutes. This freezes well. Defrost completely and bake the same as freshly made.

CREPES WITH CRAB, ALMONDS AND WATER CHESTNUTS

1 pound crabmeat (fresh, frozen or canned)
2 5-ounce cans water chestnuts
1 cup blanched almonds
1 cup chopped onions
8 tablespoons butter
½ cup white wine
1 cup thick cream sauce (page 172)
½ teaspoon ginger
½ teaspoon nutmeg
½ teaspoon black pepper
salt to taste
14–16 5-inch crepes

Flake the crabmeat and pick out the cartilage. Chop the water chestnuts and almonds to a fine dice (or grind with the coarse blade of a grinder or in a blender at the slowest speed). Cook onions in butter in a large skillet until limp and all moisture has evaporated. Add the crabmeat to the pan and stir to combine with butter. Add white wine and cook rapidly to reduce by half. Stir ginger, nutmeg and black pepper into cream sauce and add salt to taste. Mix with the crabmeat mixture and cook and stir until sauce thickens. Add chopped water chestnuts and almonds.

Put a spoonful or two of filling down the center of each crepe. Roll and place seam side down in a buttered baking dish. Bake at 375° F. for 20 minutes. This freezes well; defrost completely and bake the same as freshly made.

ALTERNATE SEASONINGS
Curry powder to taste may be used instead of or along

with the other spices. Or black pepper alone may be used.

CREPES WITH CRABMEAT IN SHRIMP SOUP

2 cans frozen shrimp soup
12 ounces crabmeat
  (fresh, frozen or
  canned)
2 tablespoons butter
1 carrot, scraped and
  chopped
1 stalk celery, cleaned
  and chopped

½ green pepper, seeded
  and chopped
¾ cup cream
2 tablespoons sherry
salt and pepper to taste
16–18 5-inch crepes

Defrost frozen shrimp soup and crabmeat, if frozen. Melt butter and when it bubbles up add finely chopped vegetables. Sauté for 2 or 3 minutes; they must remain crisp. Add crabmeat and heat just for a minute or two. Mix defrosted soup and cream in a bowl and stir until lumps are all gone. Add to crabmeat mixture, then add sherry.

Butter a baking dish and fill each crepe with a couple of spoonfuls of mixture. Roll up and turn seam side down. Some of the soup–cream mixture may be saved to spread over tops of the crepes. Heat in a 400° F. oven for 10 or 15 minutes. May be frozen and reheated after defrosting; or in a freezer-to-oven pan, may be baked for 40 minutes at 300° F. then 10–15 minutes at 400° F.

CREPES WITH CURRIED CRAB

1 pound crabmeat (fresh, frozen or canned)
4 tablespoons butter
1 medium onion, chopped
1 stalk celery, finely chopped
1 tablespoon curry powder (or to taste)
salt and pepper to taste
1 cup chicken broth
1 tablespoon cornstarch
¼ cup cream
14–16 5-inch crepes

Heat butter in a heavy skillet. Sauté the onion and celery until limp. Add curry powder and salt and pepper to taste. Cover and cook about 5 minutes. Add chicken broth, saving one tablespoon to mix with the cornstarch. When mixture comes to the boil, add the blended cornstarch. Cook until thickened. Add crabmeat and cream and cook and stir until thickened again.

Put a spoonful or two of filling down the center of each crepe. Roll and turn seam side down in a buttered baking dish. If any sauce remains it may be spread over the tops of the crepes. Bake at 375° F. for 20 minutes. This may be frozen. Defrost completely and bake the same as freshly made.

CREPES WITH CRAB AND GREEN ONIONS

2 or 3 bunches of green
   onions
2 tablespoons butter
4 or 5 mushrooms,
   thinly sliced
1 tablespoon cooking oil
1 can bamboo shoots
1 can water chestnuts
½ pound crabmeat
   (fresh, canned or
   frozen)

1 cup chicken broth
1 teaspoon soy sauce
2 teaspoons of cornstarch
   dissolved in
   1 tablespoon water
salt to taste
14–16 5-inch crepes
½ cup chopped almonds

Shred the green onions, using both the white and green parts, and sauté in the butter. Add the mushrooms. In another skillet, heat the oil and add the bamboo shoots and water chestnuts, sliced and cut again in small pieces. Stir for a minute, add the crabmeat, the onions and mushrooms and the chicken broth and soy sauce. Simmer for a minute or two and add the cornstarch dissolved in water. Cook until it thickens and add salt to taste.

Pour a spoonful or two of the mixture down the center of each crepe. Roll and turn seam side down in a buttered baking dish. Bake at 375° F. for 20 minutes. This does *not* freeze well.

CREPES WITH SHERRIED CRAB AND CELERY

3 tablespoons butter
2 slices of dry bread
   finely crumbed
   (about 1 cup)
1 cup finely chopped
   celery
¼ cup finely chopped
   onion

½ pound crabmeat
2 eggs
2 tablespoons cream
3 tablespoons sherry
salt and pepper to taste
14–16 5-inch crepes

Heat 1 tablespoon of the butter in a large skillet and brown the breadcrumbs. Turn into a bowl. Put the remaining 2 tablespoons of butter in the skillet and sauté the chopped celery and onion for 2 or 3 minutes. Add the crabmeat and cook just until heated through. Mix the eggs, cream and sherry and beat lightly. Pour over the toasted crumbs and mix well. Pour the mixture over the crab and cook only a minute or two more.

Put a spoonful or two of the mixture down the center of each crepe. Roll and turn seam side down in a buttered baking dish. Bake at 375° F. for 20 minutes. This does *not* freeze well.

CREPES WITH LOBSTER NEWBURG

2 cups lobster meat
    or part lobster and
    part other seafood
2 tablespoons butter
½ pound mushrooms,
    thinly sliced
2 cups medium cream
    sauce (page 172)

¼ cup dry sherry
3 egg yolks
½ cup cream
1 teaspoon paprika
salt and pepper to taste
2 tablespoons cognac
14–16 5-inch crepes

Cut the lobster and other seafood, if used, into small pieces. Heat the butter in a large skillet and sauté the mushrooms for 3 or 4 minutes, turning constantly. Add the lobster meat and cook only to heat through.

To 2 cups of medium cream sauce, add the sherry, stir well, then add the egg yolks blended into the cream and paprika. Pour about a third of the sauce over the lobster and mushroom mixture. Reserve the rest for topping. Check seasoning.

Put a spoonful or two of the mixture down the center of each crepe. Roll and turn seam side down in a buttered baking dish. Bake at 375° F. for 20 minutes. This freezes well. Defrost completely and bake the same as freshly made.

CREPES WITH LOBSTER IN VERMOUTH

1 pound lobster meat
2 tablespoons butter
2 tablespoons chopped
  green onions
½ cup vermouth
1½ cups cream
1 teaspoon French
  mustard
1 tablespoon cornstarch
  blended with
  1 tablespoon butter

3 tablespoons grated
  cheese
salt and black pepper to
  taste
14–16 5-inch crepes
Optional topping: grated
  cheese, buttered
  crumbs, or cream
  sauce with a little
  vermouth and nutmeg

Cut the lobster meat into small pieces. Heat the butter in a heavy saucepan and sauté the green onions until wilted but not brown. Add the vermouth and when it boils up add the cream and French mustard. Stir in the cornstarch blended with water and add salt and black pepper to taste. Cook slowly for about 10 minutes until sauce is quite thick. Add the lobster meat, stir and blend in the cheese. Cool slightly.

Place a spoonful or two of filling down the center of each crepe. Roll and turn seam side down in a buttered baking dish. The top of the crepes may be sprinkled with cheese or buttered crumbs or cream sauce to which vermouth and a little nutmeg has been added. Bake at 375° F. for 20 minutes. This freezes well; defrost completely and bake the same as freshly made.

CREPES WITH LOBSTER CANTONESE

1 pound lobster meat
½ pound ground pork
2 cloves of garlic, minced
1 teaspoon minced fresh
   ginger (if available)
3 tablespoons peanut oil
2 tablespoons dry sherry

1 tablespoon soy sauce
1 tablespoon cornstarch
   mixed with
   1 tablespoon water
¾ cup chicken broth
2 beaten eggs
14–16 5-inch crepes

Cut lobster meat into small pieces. Combine pork with garlic and fresh ginger. Heat oil in large skillet over high heat and add pork mixture, browning and stirring for 3 or 4 minutes. Add lobster mixed with sherry and soy sauce. Mix cornstarch with water. Add hot chicken broth to lobster–pork mixture. Blend in cornstarch and stir until sauce is thickened and clear. Stir in the beaten eggs and stir until eggs just set.

Put a spoonful or two of filling down the center of each crepe, roll and turn seam side down in a buttered baking dish. Bake for 20 minutes at 375° F. This does *not* freeze well.

CREPES WITH PINK SHRIMPS

1½ pounds shrimp,
  cooked and peeled
4 tablespoons butter
1 medium onion,
  finely chopped
½ pound mushrooms,
  chopped
1 teaspoon soy sauce

2 tablespoons tomato
  sauce or catsup
1 teaspoon paprika
1 cup sour cream
2 tablespoons chopped
  parsley
salt and pepper to taste
14–16 5-inch crepes

Cut shrimp into 4 or 5 pieces each. Heat butter to bubbling in a large skillet, add the onion and sauté until clear. Add mushrooms and sauté 3 or 4 minutes until limp. Add shrimp and stir to coat with butter and juices. Mix the soy sauce, tomato sauce or catsup and paprika into the sour cream and spoon into the pan with the shrimp. Add chopped parsley and salt and pepper to taste.

Spread a spoonful or two of shrimp mixture along the center of each crepe. Roll and place seam side down in a buttered baking dish. Brush the sauce that remains in the pan over the tops of the crepes. Bake at 375° F. for 20 minutes. This freezes well. Defrost completely and bake the same as freshly made.

VARIATION

Any shellfish is good with this sauce. Half shrimp and half scallops are a good combination.

CREPES WITH SHRIMP CREOLE

1½ pounds shrimp,
   cooked, and shelled
4 tablespoons butter
½ cup finely chopped
   onion
1 green pepper, chopped
salt and pepper to taste

4 cups tomato sauce,
   fresh, page 175,
   your own or canned
14–16 5-inch crepes
½ cup grated Parmesan
   or Romano cheese for
   topping

Use fresh, canned or frozen shrimp. To precook fresh shrimp in the shell, add half a lemon, a piece of celery, a carrot, a teaspoon of mixed herbs and one bay leaf to sufficient water to cover the shrimp. After the water comes to a boil, put in the shrimp and cook gently for five minutes after water begins to boil again. Shell shrimp and cut out black vein along top.

Heat butter in a large skillet, add chopped onion and green pepper and sauté about 10 minutes. Cut shrimp into slices about ½-inch thick, add to the onion and green pepper and cook for a minute or two, stirring to coat the shrimp with butter. Add 1½ cups of the tomato sauce and cook another 2 or 3 minutes. Cool slightly.

Put a spoonful or two of the filling down the middle of each crepe. Roll and place seam side down in a buttered baking dish. Cover with the remainder of the tomato sauce and the grated cheese. Bake at 375° F. for 20 minutes. This freezes well. Defrost completely and bake the same as freshly made.

CREPES WITH SHRIMP AND WATER CHESTNUTS

2 scallions
2 tablespoons butter
1 pound shrimp, cooked
   and peeled
¼ pound mushrooms,
   finely chopped
1 can water chestnuts,
   chopped

1 cup thick cream sauce
   (page 172)
2 tablespoons white wine
salt and pepper
14–16 5-inch crepes

Clean and shred scallions. Heat butter in skillet until it bubbles up. Add scallions and sauté until they are wilted. Cut shrimp into one-third-inch slices and cook only until they are coated with butter. Add mushrooms and cook 2 minutes and add water chestnuts, then 1 cup thick cream sauce thinned with 2 tablespoons of white wine. Season to taste. Heat only until well mixed.

Cool and fill crepes, putting a tablespoon or two of filling along the center of crepe. Roll and turn seam side down in a buttered baking dish. Bake 10–15 minutes in a 400° F. oven. This will serve 4 or 5. The filled crepes may be frozen, defrosted completely and baked the same as freshly made. Or if a freezer-to-oven pan is used, bake 40 minutes at 350° F., then 10–15 minutes at 400° F. For a richer dish, cream sauce may be poured over the top of the crepes and a sprinkling of cheese added.

CREPES WITH OYSTERS AND HAM

1 *pint fresh shucked*
    oysters or 2 8-ounce
    cans oysters
¼ *pound ham*
4 *tablespoons butter*
¼ *pound mushrooms,*
    thinly sliced
2 *tablespoons flour*
chicken broth or fish stock
    —up to 1 cup

½ *cup heavy cream*
¼ *cup breadcrumbs*
2 *tablespoons parsley*
½ *teaspoon nutmeg*
black pepper; salt, if
    needed
14–16 *5-inch crepes*

Strain oysters and save the liquor. Cut ham into half-inch dice. Melt butter in heavy pan and sauté mushrooms until limp. Sprinkle flour over the mushrooms and butter and stir and brown only slightly. Add fish stock or chicken broth to oyster liquor to make 1½ cups and stir into the mushrooms and flour. Cook until liquid thickens, then add heavy cream and cook until it boils up. Add breadcrumbs, oysters, ham, parsley, nutmeg and black pepper to taste. Check for salt, but none may be needed depending on the saltiness of both ham and oysters.

Put a tablespoon or two of filling down the center of each crepe, roll and turn seam side down in a buttered baking dish. Bake at 375° F. for 20 minutes. This does *not* freeze well.

CREPES WITH OYSTERS ROCKEFELLER

1 *pint shucked oysters or*
  2 8-ounce cans oysters
8 *tablespoons butter*
¼ *cup finely chopped*
  shallots or scallions
1 *small clove garlic,*
  minced
¼ *cup chopped celery*
¼ *cup chopped parsley*
1 *cup chopped spinach,*
  fresh or frozen

¼ *cup anisette or Pernod*
1 *teaspoon Worcester-*
  shire sauce
salt and black pepper and
  cayenne to taste
14–16 *5-inch crepes*
½ *cup buttered bread-*
  crumbs

Drain the oysters. Heat the butter to bubbling in a skillet and add shallots or scallions and the garlic. Cook until wilted but do not brown. Add the celery and cook for a minute or two, then add parsley and spinach. If the spinach is fresh cook only until wilted but still green. If frozen spinach is used, cook separately and drain before adding. Add the anisette or Pernod and the Worcestershire sauce. Put the sauce in a blender and blend about a minute until pureed. (A fine food mill can be used instead of a blender.) Taste for seasoning. Add the oysters to the sauce.

Put a spoonful or two of the filling down the center of each crepe. Roll and turn seam side down in a buttered baking dish. Sprinkle crumbs over top and bake at 400° F. for 15 minutes. This does *not* freeze well.

CREPES WITH CLAMS MONTAUK

2 10-ounce cans clams,
   minced, or 1 pint fresh
   clams finely chopped
½ pound salt pork, diced
2 tablespoons butter
2 onions, chopped
2 carrots, chopped
2 stalks celery, chopped

2 fresh tomatoes, chopped
salt and pepper and
   cayenne to taste
1 tablespoon cornstarch
chicken or fish stock as
   needed (about ½ cup)
14–16 5-inch crepes

Drain the clams and save the juice. Fry the salt pork in the butter in a heavy saucepan. Remove when golden and add the finely chopped onions, carrots and celery. (At Montauk they grind the vegetables in a coarse-bladed grinder.) Sauté only until coated and add the tomatoes. Cook for about 20 minutes or until vegetables are medium soft. Add clams and stir and cook for a minute or two. Mix the cornstarch with part of the reserved clam juice. Add the remainder to the stew and when it begins to simmer add the cornstarch; blend and stir until thickened. Add chicken or fish stock, and salt, pepper and cayenne to taste.

Fill each crepe with a spoonful or two of filling. Roll and place seam side down in a buttered baking dish. Bake for 20 minutes at 375° F. These freeze well. Defrost completely and bake the same as freshly made.

CREPES WITH CLAMS NEW ENGLAND

¼ *pound salt pork, diced*	¼ *cup breadcrumbs*
2 *tablespoons butter*	1 *cup milk*
2 *onions, chopped*	1 *cup cream*
2 *10-ounce cans of*	½ *teaspoon nutmeg*
chopped clams	*salt and pepper to taste*
2 *diced potatoes*	14–16 *5-inch crepes*

Sauté the salt pork in the butter in a heavy-bottomed saucepan until crisp and golden. Remove from pan and add chopped onions. Brown lightly and cook until soft. Drain the clams and cook the diced potatoes in the clam juice until potatoes are just tender—about 10 minutes. Add potatoes and juice to the onions, return the salt pork to the pan and stir in the breadcrumbs. Cook until quite thick and add milk and cream slowly, allowing sauce to thicken up after each addition. If sauce is too thin, cook a little longer or add more breadcrumbs. Finally stir in the clams. Add salt, pepper and nutmeg to taste.

Put a spoonful or two of the filling down the center of each crepe. Roll and turn seam side down and place in a buttered baking dish. Spread remaining sauce over tops of crepes. Bake at 375° F. for 20 minutes. This freezes well. Defrost completely and bake the same as freshly made.

CREPES WITH MUSSELS

1½ cups cooked mussels
  (clams may be
  substituted)
¼ pound mushrooms,
  chopped
2 tablespoons butter
10 medium shrimp,
  finely chopped
2 tablespoons liquid from
  mussels

1 cup cream
2 teaspoons cornstarch
  dissolved in
  1 tablespoon water
4 crushed crackers
salt and pepper to taste
juice of half a lemon
14–16 5-inch crepes

Fresh mussels should stand for a couple of hours in cold water to release their sand. They need to be well scrubbed. Steam them in a mixture of soup vegetables and white wine until their shells open. Otherwise, use canned mussels or substitute clams. Drain and reserve the juice.

Sauté mushrooms in the butter in a large skillet. Add the finely chopped shrimp to the pan, then add mussels or clams and 2 tablespoons of drained liquid. (The rest of the liquid can be frozen and used to poach fish.) Add the cream and bring to a simmer. Blend the water into the cornstarch and add to the pan sauce. Cook until it thickens and add the cracker crumbs. Stir well. Add salt and pepper to taste. Sprinkle with lemon juice and cool slightly.

Put a spoonful or two of the mixture down the center of each crepe. Roll and turn seam side down in a buttered baking dish. Bake at 375° F. for 20 minutes.

This freezes well. Defrost completely before baking and bake the same as freshly made.

CREPES WITH SOLE VERONICA

2 shallots or green onions,
  chopped fine
2 tablespoons butter
1 cup chicken broth
  or fish stock
½ cup white wine
1½ pounds fillet of sole
  (or flounder)

1 cup white seedless
  grapes
1 tablespoon cornstarch
½ cup heavy cream
1 egg yolk
salt and pepper to taste
14–16 5-inch crepes

Sauté the shallots or green onions in the butter and add the chicken broth or stock and the white wine and put in the fillets of sole. Simmer for 8 or 10 minutes or until fish turns opaque white and flakes easily. Turn if necessary. Remove the fish and boil the stock down to about half its original quantity. Combine the cornstarch with a little of the cream and add to the boiling stock, stirring all the while. Lower heat.

Combine the egg yolk with the rest of the cream and stir in off heat. Return to low heat and cook until the sauce thickens. Add the grapes (if canned, drain), the fish broken up and cook only until blended. Add salt and pepper to taste.

Put a spoonful or two of the filling down the center of each crepe. Roll and turn seam side down in a buttered baking dish. Spread remaining sauce over each crepe or combine remaining sauce with a ½ cup of heavy cream whipped and spread over the crepes. Bake at 375° F. for 20 minutes. This freezes well. Defrost completely and bake the same as freshly made.

CREPES WITH SOLE AND MARGUERY SAUCE

1 pound fillet of sole
  or flounder
1 cup fish or chicken stock
1 tablespoon grated onion
2 egg whites
¼ cup heavy cream
salt and pepper to taste
speck of cayenne
14–16 5-inch crepes

Sauce:
2 cups of medium cream
  sauce (page 172)
2 egg yolks
¼ cup heavy cream
juice of one lemon
can of tiny shrimp
¼ pound sliced
  mushrooms cooked in
  2 tablespoons butter
salt and pepper to taste

Cook the fillets of sole or flounder in the stock with the grated onion. Grind cooked fish in food chopper with the finest blade or put in blender with a little of the cooking stock. Beat egg whites until stiff. Beat cream until stiff. Mix with the fish, adding seasonings.

Put a spoonful or two of the filling down the center of each crepe. Roll and turn seam side down in a buttered baking dish.

Make a cream sauce using fish stock for part of the liquid. Add egg yolks beaten slightly with cream, lemon juice, tiny shrimp and mushrooms sautéed in butter and salt and pepper to taste. Pour over the tops of crepes. Bake in a 350° F. oven for 20 minutes. Raise heat to 400° F. and bake for another 5 minutes. This does *not* freeze well.

CREPES WITH TUNA FISH, BLACK OLIVES AND MUSHROOMS

2 7-ounce cans tuna fish,
drained
2 tablespoons butter
½ pound mushrooms,
chopped
½ cup chopped onions or
scallions
2 stalks celery, chopped

½ cup finely chopped
black olives
¼ teaspoon thyme
salt and pepper to taste
2 cups Mornay sauce
(page 173)
14–16 5-inch crepes

Thoroughly drain the cans of tuna fish. Set tuna aside.
Melt butter in a large skillet. When it is bubbling, add
mushrooms, onions or scallions and celery and sauté
until limp and golden. Add tuna fish, olives, thyme,
salt and pepper to taste. Add enough Mornay sauce to
hold mixture together.

Place a spoonful or two of the mixture down the
center of each crepe. Roll and turn seam side down in
a buttered baking dish. Cover the crepes with remaining Mornay sauce. Bake at 375° F. for 15–20 minutes.
This freezes well. Defrost completely and bake the
same as freshly made.

CREPES WITH SALMON AND MUSHROOMS

2 cups salmon, canned or
  freshly cooked and
  flaked
4 tablespoons minced
  shallots or green onions
½ pound mushrooms,
  diced

4 tablespoons butter
1–2 cups Mornay sauce
  (page 173)
salt and pepper to taste
½ cup grated Parmesan or
  Swiss cheese
14–16 5-inch crepes

If you are using fresh salmon, poach it first; then cool and flake it. If you are using canned salmon, pick it over to remove any bones and flake it also.

Sauté minced shallots or onions and diced mushrooms in butter until limp and golden. Add the salmon to the sautéed vegetables. Use about half of the Mornay sauce and add it to the salmon mixture. Season to taste.

Fill each crepe with one or two spoonfuls of the mixture, roll and turn seam side down in a buttered baking dish. Spread remaining sauce over the top and sprinkle with grated cheese. Bake at 375° F. for 20 minutes. May be frozen without the cheese. Defrost completely, adding cheese just before baking, and bake the same as freshly made.

Crepes Cannelloni and Pizza Crepes

CREPES CANNELLONI WITH CHICKEN AND SPINACH

3 chicken livers
1 cup cooked chicken
2 tablespoons butter
2 tablespoons chopped onion
1 cup chopped spinach, cooked and well drained

¼ cup chicken broth
½ cup thick cream sauce (page 172)
2 tablespoons grated cheese
14–16 5-inch crepes

Topping:
2 cups medium cream sauce (page 172)

½ cup grated cheese

Wash, dry and remove connective tissue from chicken livers. Cut into pieces. Cut up cooked chicken into moderately small pieces. Melt butter in a large skillet, add chopped onions and livers and sauté for 2 or 3 minutes until no blood comes from the livers. Add cut-up chicken, the spinach and chicken broth. Put through the grinder with the finest blade or blend at low to medium speed in blender. Add ½ cup cream sauce and cheese.

Butter a baking pan. Put 2 spoonfuls of mixture down the center of each crepe, roll and turn seam side down. Cover with cream sauce and sprinkle with grated cheese. Freezes well. In a freezer-to-oven pan bake 40 minutes at 300° F. then 15 minutes at 400° F. Or defrost completely and bake the same as freshly made.

CREPES CANNELLONI WITH CHICKEN, HAM AND MUSHROOMS

½ pound chicken, raw or cooked (2 boned breasts)
½ pound ham
½ pound mushrooms
2 tablespoons butter
2 tablespoons oil
¼ cup chicken broth
2 tablespoons Madeira wine (sherry can be substituted)

2 eggs
½ cup cream
¼ cup grated cheese (Romano, Parmesan or part Swiss)
salt and pepper to taste
14–16 5-inch crepes

Topping:
2 cups medium cream sauce (page 172)

¼ cup grated cheese

Cut chicken, ham and mushrooms into pieces and sauté in butter and oil. (If chicken is raw, sauté it first for 3 minutes, then add ham and mushrooms.) Cook over medium heat for 3 or 4 minutes longer, add chicken broth and Madeira and cook another 3 or 4 minutes. Put meat and mushroom mixture through meat grinder using finest blade or in blender at low to medium speed. Beat eggs, add cream and ¼ cup grated cheese and beat again. Beat into chicken mixture.

Then fill each crepe generously with mixture, roll up and turn seam side down in a baking pan which has been spread with a little of the cream sauce. Pour remaining cream sauce over the top of the crepes and sprinkle with cheese. Bake 20 minutes in a 400° F. oven. This freezes well. If completely defrosted bake the same as fresh. In a freezer-to-oven pan bake 40 minutes at 300° F. then 20 minutes at 400° F.

CREPES CANNELLONI SUPREME

¼ pound beef
¼ pound veal
¼ pound pork
¼ pound ham
½ cup cooked chicken
4 tablespoons butter
   (half stick)
½ cup chopped
   mushrooms
½ cup finely sliced onion

1 tomato, cut in pieces
½ package frozen spinach
   or ¼ pound fresh
½ cup cream sauce
salt and pepper to taste
1 cup grated cheese,
   Parmesan or Romano
   or part Swiss
1 egg
16–18 5-inch crepes

Topping:
2 cups medium cream
   sauce (page 172)

2 cups tomato sauce
1 cup grated cheese

If the meats are uncooked they should be ground and sautéed. Be sure that the fresh pork is well cooked. If the meats are leftover and already cooked, they should be cut in small pieces along with the chicken.

MAIN COURSE CREPES / 123

Melt butter, sauté mushrooms and onion for about 5 minutes, add the cut-up tomato and cook 2 or 3 minutes more. Frozen spinach should be defrosted; fresh spinach cleaned and cooked in the water that clings to the leaves, then drained. Put everything through the grinder with the fine blade or on medium-high speed in a blender. Add the cream sauce to the other ingredients while blending or if ground, after grinding, then the grated cheese and the egg. Mix well. Mixture should be fairly stiff but if it is too stiff, add more cream sauce or a little plain cream.

Put 2 spoonfuls down the center of each crepe. Roll and turn seam side down in a buttered baking dish. Top with cream sauce and then tomato sauce, or put the sauces on in a ribbon effect. Sprinkle with grated cheese and bake at 400° F. for 20 minutes. This freezes well, with or without sauce which may be added before baking. It is better to defrost completely and bake the same as freshly made.

This is an elaborate recipe but it is also an elastic one. You can cut down on the number of meats, or cut out the spinach if there's none around. It is better if at least one of the meats is freshly cooked.

Cannelloni made with crepes is not an innovation. It is considered the most delicate form of Cannelloni. Good Italian restaurants use larger crepes and square them off to a 4 × 4 size. This seems an unnecessary refinement, but if you like a neat bundle, the scraps can always be cut into strips and used for soup.

BASIC PIZZA CREPES

2 cups thick tomato sauce
2 tablespoons olive oil
   or cooking oil
1 cup chopped onions
salt and pepper to taste

2 cups grated or shredded
   cheese (Parmesan,
   Swiss, mozzarella)
oregano or basil
16–18 5-inch crepes

Topping:
2 cups thinned tomato
   sauce

½ cup grated cheese

Use canned tomato sauce, fresh tomato sauce (page 175) or your own recipe. Heat oil in skillet and cook onions until they are limp but not browned. Add tomato sauce and grated or shredded cheese of your preference or a mixture. If sauce is not highly seasoned, add oregano, basil, salt and pepper.

Butter a baking dish, put 2 spoonfuls of cooled filling down the center of each crepe, roll up and turn seam side down. Cover with 2 cups thinned tomato sauce and sprinkle with grated cheese. Bake in a hot oven, 450° F. for 10 or 15 minutes. If cheese does not brown sufficiently, run under a broiler for a minute or two. May be frozen with or without topping, defrosted and baked the same as fresh. If you use the large 8-inch crepes, spread a little of the filling on one, and instead of rolling the crepes, stack them one on another with filling between each one. Top off with a bit more sauce and grated cheese and cook as above.

VARIATIONS

MUSHROOM PIZZA CREPES
Sauté ¼ pound of sliced mushrooms with the onions.

BLACK OLIVE PIZZA CREPES
Add 1 cup sliced black olives with the tomato sauce.

SAUSAGE PIZZA CREPES
Slice ½ pound of Italian hot or sweet sausage in quarter-inch slices; sauté with onions.

ANCHOVY PIZZA CREPES
Add one can of drained anchovies with the tomato sauce.

BEST PIZZA CREPES
Sauté ¼ pound of sliced mushrooms with the onions, add ¼ pound of sliced Italian hot sausage to the skillet; cook for a minute then add ½ cup pitted black olives with the tomato sauce along with one clove finely chopped garlic.

Crepes
Filled with
Vegetables

When you serve crepes filled with vegetables, it is not nec-
essary to serve potatoes or any starchy dish. Since most
crepes filled with vegetables are in a rich sauce, they go
best with roast and broiled meats. Many of the vegetable
crepes can also be served for lunch as a light main dish
with a salad that can range from a mixed green salad to a
chef's salad or even a chicken salad. One filled crepe will
usually be enough as a side dish with meat; two or three
may be needed for a luncheon main course.

CREPES WITH ASPARAGUS IN
MORNAY SAUCE

1–1½ pounds asparagus
6–8 5-inch crepes flavored
   with grated lemon rind

1½ cups Mornay sauce
   (page 173)

Clean and trim asparagus; cut to size of crepes—5
inches long for 5-inch crepes. Precook in a large quantity of boiling water until just tender—they will cook
again in the oven.

Butter a small baking dish. Put 3 to 5 asparagus depending on size down the middle of each crepe; put a spoonful or two of Mornay sauce on top of the asparagus and roll up and turn seam side down. Pour the rest of the sauce over the filled crepes and bake in a 400° F. oven for 15 minutes. These may be made ahead and kept in the refrigerator until time to bake. Serves 6 accompanying a roast, broiled steak or fish, 2 or 3 as a main course with fruit and salad. Broccoli may be used instead of asparagus.

VARIATION

CREPES WITH ASPARAGUS AND MELTED CHEESE
Prepare the same as asparagus in Mornay sauce, but omit the sauce and put a thin slice of cheese, Swiss or cheddar, over each bundle of asparagus before rolling the crepe and sprinkle tops with grated cheese. This can also be used for broccoli.

CREPES WITH GREEN BEANS, MUSHROOMS AND SOUR CREAM

1 pound green beans
¼ pound mushrooms, sliced
2 tablespoons butter
½ cup sour cream
salt and pepper to taste
6–8 5-inch crepes
½ cup fine breadcrumbs

Cook the beans, slivered, French style, in boiling water until just tender. Drain. Brown mushrooms in 2 tablespoons of butter. Add the sour cream and blend well. Combine with the beans.

Butter a small baking dish and put two spoonfuls

of beans down the center of each crepe, roll and turn seam side down. Sprinkle with breadcrumbs and bake for 15 minutes at 400° F. Serves 6 accompanying a roast, broiled fish or meat. This does *not* freeze well.

Crepes with Green Beans Mediterranean

1 pound green beans
½ cup chicken broth
4 tablespoons butter
1 onion, finely chopped
1 clove garlic, minced
1 green pepper,
   finely chopped

2 tomatoes peeled
   and chopped
1 tablespoon chopped
   parsley
2 teaspoons cornstarch
   dissolved in
   1 tablespoon water
10–12 5-inch crepes

If the beans are young and tender they may be left whole. Otherwise, cut in one-inch pieces on a slant. Cook beans in chicken broth until barely tender. Drain but save the cooking liquid. Heat butter until it bubbles in a large skillet, add the onion and garlic and cook until limp, then the green pepper, tomatoes and parsley and cook on medium-high heat until most of the liquid evaporates. Add the cooking liquid from the beans and when it boils up add the cornstarch dissolved in water and cook until sauce thickens. Combine with the beans.

Put a spoonful or two of beans and sauce down the center of each crepe, roll up and turn seam side down in a buttered baking dish. Brush the tops with the sauce that remains in the pan. Bake at 375° F. for 20 minutes. This does *not* freeze well, but may be made ahead of time. This goes well with baked or broiled fish.

CREPES WITH GREEN BEANS CHINESE STYLE

½ pound green beans
1 tablespoon butter
1 can water chestnuts,
  sliced
1 cup chicken broth
salt and pepper to taste

2 teaspoons cornstarch
  dissolved in
  1 tablespoon water
½ cup slivered toasted
  almonds
6–8 5-inch crepes

Cut the beans in thin, slanted sections and parboil for 5 minutes in boiling water. Drain. Melt butter and when it bubbles, toss in the beans and stir over high heat. Lower heat and add sliced water chestnuts and then chicken broth. Season to taste. Add the cornstarch dissolved in water and cook and stir until it thickens and the sauce becomes clear. Add the slivered almonds and cool slightly.

Butter a small baking dish. Put two spoonfuls of the bean mixture down the center of each crepe, roll and turn seam side down. Bake in a 400° F. oven for 15 minutes. This does *not* freeze well.

CREPES WITH CELERY AND HAM

3 tablespoons butter
3 cups celery, cut in
   1-inch sticks
¼ pound ham, cut in
   cubes
¾–1 cup chicken broth

¼ cup cream
1 teaspoon cornstarch
½ cup slivered almonds
melted butter
16 5-inch crepes

Melt butter in skillet, add celery and ham and sauté without browning for five minutes. Add ¾ cup chicken broth and simmer until celery is just tender and most of the broth is gone. Add more broth if necessary. Mix cream with cornstarch. Stir into celery and ham mixture and cook for 2 or 3 minutes more, until thickened.

Butter a baking pan. Fill each crepe with a spoonful or two of celery mixture, roll and turn seam down in the pan. Sprinkle slivered almonds and melted butter over top. Bake in a 375° F. oven for 15–20 minutes. Serve with roast chicken or as a main luncheon dish with fruit salad. This does *not* freeze well.

CREPES WITH MUSHROOMS IN BROWN SAUCE

¼ pound butter
1 medium onion,
   finely chopped
1 carrot, finely chopped
1 thin slice boiled ham,
   diced
salt and pepper to taste
1½ pounds mushrooms,
   chopped

4 tablespoons flour
1½ cups brown stock
   or bouillon
2 tablespoons red wine
   or Madeira (optional)
extra butter
16–18 5-inch crepes, plain
   or made with stock

Melt a stick of butter in a large skillet. When butter bubbles up add chopped onion and carrot and the thin slice of ham also cut in small dice. Add salt and pepper to taste. Use medium-high heat and allow the vegetables and ham to brown but not burn; add mushrooms and cook until mushrooms begin to brown. When all the pan juices have evaporated, sprinkle 4 tablespoons of flour over the pan and stir and cook until the flour also begins to brown. Add the brown stock or bouillon and cook and stir for about 5 minutes. Add wine and cook until the sauce is quite thick.

Butter a baking dish and put a spoonful or two of filling down the center of each crepe, roll and turn seam side down. Brush tops of crepes with a little melted butter and bake 15–20 minutes at 375° F. This freezes well, but it is best defrosted completely and baked the same as fresh. This filling may be frozen by itself and defrosted quickly in a double boiler, the crepes then filled and baked as usual.

Serve with roast beef, steak or plain pot roast instead

of potatoes or noodles along with a green salad or vegetable. Allow 3 crepes per person as a main dish, 2 as a side dish.

CREPES WITH MUSHROOMS IN CHEESE SAUCE

3 tablespoons butter
1 pound mushrooms, sliced or quartered
1 medium onion, chopped
2 cups medium cream sauce (page 172)
½ cup grated cheese (Romano, Parmesan, Swiss or sharp white cheddar)
salt and pepper to taste
12–16 5-inch crepes

Melt butter and when it bubbles add the onion and cook until limp but not brown. Add mushrooms and cook until they change color and are limp. Add a little less than 1 cup of cream sauce and 1 tablespoon of the grated cheese.

Grease a flat casserole or baking dish. Put a table-spoon or two of filling down the center of each crepe, roll and turn seam side down. Add the rest of the grated cheese to the remaining cream sauce and pour over the filled crepes. Extra cheese may be sprinkled on top. Bake in a hot oven, 400° F. for 15 minutes. If not brown and bubbling, run under the broiler for 2 or 3 minutes. This freezes well. If completely defrosted bake the same as fresh. In a freezer-to-oven pan bake 40 minutes at 300° F. then 20 minutes at 400° F.

CREPES WITH MUSHROOMS IN SOUR CREAM

¼ pound butter
2 medium onions,
   chopped
1½ pounds mushrooms
salt and pepper to taste
1 cup sour cream

2 teaspoons dry mustard
2 teaspoons soy sauce
1 tablespoon tomato
   catsup
16 5-inch crepes

Melt the butter in a large skillet. When it is bubbling put in the chopped onions and sauté until limp. Meanwhile cut cleaned trimmed mushrooms in half and then slice the other way. (If mushrooms are large, cut in three before slicing.) Add to the onions in the pan and sauté for 4 or 5 minutes until they begin to change color.

To the cup of sour cream add the dry mustard, soy sauce and catsup. Stir into mushroom mixture and cook 3 or 4 minutes over low heat until well blended and hot.

Keep crepes hot in oven if freshly made, defrost and warm in oven if frozen. Heat a serving dish, fill crepes with the mushroom mixture and bring to the table. This filling may be frozen and defrosted in the top of a double boiler.

This will serve 6 as a luncheon main course with a fresh green vegetable or a fruit salad, 8 as an accompaniment for any roast, broiled meat or fish.

CREPES FILLED WITH SPINACH AND HAM SOUFFLÉ

¾ pound spinach or
  1 package frozen
  spinach (chopped)
1 cup ground cooked ham
4 tablespoons butter
4 tablespoons flour
½ teaspoon freshly grated
  black pepper
½ teaspoon nutmeg
salt to taste

2 cups milk or part milk
  and part stock
½ cup cream
½ cup grated Parmesan
  or Swiss cheese
4 egg yolks
5 egg whites
16 5-inch crepes

Cook spinach, if fresh, quickly in water that clings to the leaves after it has been washed. Chop fine, or use frozen chopped spinach. Grind cooked ham and add to spinach. Melt butter, add flour, pepper, nutmeg and salt and stir over a low flame until well blended.

Heat the milk or stock and milk and add all at once off the fire. Cook until well thickened, add cream and cook on a reduced flame for 15 or 20 minutes, then add grated cheese. Pour about a ¼ of the mixture into the spinach and stir well. Beat egg yolks lightly and add to spinach mixture then beat egg whites until stiff and fold in.

Butter a baking dish. Put a spoonful or two of the mixture down the center of each crepe, roll and turn seam side down. Pour remaining soufflé mixture over filled crepes and bake in a 375° F. oven for 25 minutes. This does *not* freeze well.

CREPES WITH SPINACH AND COTTAGE CHEESE

2 tablespoons minced   1 egg
  shallots or scallions   pinch nutmeg
1 tablespoon butter   salt and pepper to taste
1 pound fresh spinach or   1 cup Mornay Sauce
  1 package frozen   (page 173)
  chopped spinach   12–14 5-inch crepes
1 cup cottage cheese

Sauté the shallots or scallions in butter until golden
and limp. Cook the fresh spinach in the water that
clings to the leaves after washing, or cook frozen spinach until just defrosted; drain thoroughly. Chop the
fresh spinach after cooking. Mix cottage cheese with
the sautéed shallots, the egg and the cooked, chopped
spinach; add seasonings. Add about half of the sauce
to the spinach–cheese mixture.

Fill each crepe with a spoonful or two of filling, roll
and place seam side down in a buttered baking dish.
Cover with the remaining sauce and bake at 400° F.
about 15–20 minutes until hot and bubbly. May be
frozen if frozen spinach is not used. Defrost completely
and bake the same as freshly made.

STUFFED ZUCCHINI IN CREPES

6 zucchini about 5 inches
    long or 3 larger ones
2 tablespoons olive oil
2 tablespoons butter
2 scallions, chopped
¼ pound mushrooms,
    chopped
¼ cup dry breadcrumbs
2 tablespoons fresh
    parsley, chopped

1 medium tomato,
    finely chopped
½ cup tomato juice
2 tablespoons grated
    Parmesan cheese
salt and pepper to taste
12 crepes made with
    herbs or herbs and
    cheese (page 30)

Topping:
2 tablespoons bread-
    crumbs
2 tablespoons Parmesan
    cheese

1 tablespoon butter

Clean and lightly scrape the outside of the zucchini. Cut off ends. If the zucchini are small, cut in half lengthwise and scoop out the seeds and a little of the pulp. If they are large, cut them lengthwise, then crosswise as well to have 12 pieces. Put 2 tablespoons of olive oil in a large skillet and sauté the zucchini quickly in the oil, turning over once or twice. Remove from pan and put them in salted boiling water to cover and cook for 10 minutes, or until fork tender but not mushy.

While they are cooking, add 2 tablespoons of butter to the oil in the skillet and sauté the chopped scallions and mushrooms for 3–4 minutes. Add ¼ cup dry breadcrumbs, stir a few times then add chopped parsley and tomato. Add the tomato juice and cook until it thickens. Add the grated cheese and salt and pepper to taste.

Drain the zucchini and put a piece on each crepe. Fill the centers with the mushroom and tomato sauce and roll the crepe around the filled zucchini, seam side down. Brush tops with butter and sprinkle with cheese and crumbs. Bake at 375° F. for 20 minutes. Freezes well, but should not be held for more than a week or two.

Dessert Crepes

Throughout Europe, from Sweden and Denmark to Austria and Hungary, dessert crepes are a favorite way to end a meal, whether they are simply folded and sprinkled with confectioner's sugar as in the street stands in Paris or mated with lingonberries as in Denmark or with apricots as in Czechoslovakia. There are baked crepes and rolled crepes, stacked crepes, crepes filled with ice cream, pastry cream or fresh fruit or preserves and, most spectacular of all, crepes flamed with brandy.

For Basic Dessert Crepes and variations, see pages 31–34.

CREPES WITH CHOCOLATE MOUSSE

6 ounces semisweet
    chocolate
3 tablespoons sugar
3 tablespoons water

3 egg yolks well beaten
1½ cups heavy cream,
    whipped
12 dessert crepes

Melt the chocolate and sugar and water until smooth and thick in a heavy saucepan over low heat or in a double boiler to prevent burning. Remove from heat and cool for a few minutes. Add the beaten egg yolks a little at a time. Let mixture cool at room temperature. Do not refrigerate. Stir now and then as mixture cools. When quite cool, whip the cream until stiff and blend it into the chocolate mixture.

Cool crepes before filling. Put a spoonful or two of filling down the center of each crepe. Roll and place seam side down on serving plate. This freezes well. Defrost completely and serve.

CREPES FILLED WITH RHUBARB

4 cups cut-up rhubarb (about 1 pound)	1 tablespoon butter, softened
2 cups sugar	2 egg yolks
4 teaspoons cornstarch	14–16 dessert crepes

Cut rhubarb into ½-inch pieces. Put into the top of a double boiler over boiling water with 1 cup of the sugar. Cook, stirring occasionally until sugar melts and rhubarb begins to soften—about 10 minutes. Meanwhile mix the rest of the sugar with the cornstarch, soft butter and egg yolks, creaming together until well blended. Add to the rhubarb mixture a spoonful at a time, mixing in well. Put pan over direct low heat and cook for another 5 minutes, stirring often until mixture thickens. Cool.

Then fill 14–16 5-inch crepes. Put into a buttered baking pan and slip under the broiler for about 5 minutes. Watch carefully that they don't burn and serve immediately. Serves 4–6. Rhubarb crepes may be served with whipped cream or custard sauce if you wish. These will freeze well but should be thoroughly defrosted before heating.

ORANGE CREPES

8 large oranges peeled
  and sliced
grated rind and juice of
  1 lemon
1 cup sugar

2 tablespoons cornstarch
grated rind and juice of
  2 oranges
2 tablespoons butter
16 5-inch dessert crepes

Cut the sliced oranges into pieces, removing the center membrane. Combine the lemon juice and rind in a small saucepan. Mix the sugar, cornstarch and orange juice and rind and blend into the juices in the saucepan. Put over low heat, stirring constantly until it thickens. Add the cut-up oranges and the butter and cook and stir until the oranges are heated through and the sauce thickens again. Cool.

Butter a baking pan and put a couple of spoonfuls of the orange mixture on each crepe, saving some of the sauce. Roll up crepes and turn seam side down in a baking pan. Pour the reserved juice over the top. Just before serving, put into a hot oven (400° F.) for about 10 minutes or put under the broiler, watching carefully so they do not burn.

Crepes Tarts

Crepes tarts, like Crepes quiche, are baked in muffin tins in the oven. They have sweet fillings that are thick and cold or chilled before filling and baking. Place each crepe centered over a muffin cup. Put 2 spoonfuls of filling in the center and with the forefinger and thumb of each hand push in the sides of the crepes and gently lower them into the muffin cup. They will make a tulip or four-leaf-clover shape. The muffin tins should *not* be buttered. Bake in a low oven—300° F.—on the lowest possible rung in order to get the bottom crisp. Baking time depends partly on the filling but will average around 30 minutes. They can be served warm or cold. They can be reheated but do not keep well for more than a day. However, they may be frozen. Defrost completely and reheat in a moderate oven (350° F.) for 10 minutes.

Any sweet or plain crepe recipe can be used for crepes tarts, but here is one that is especially good:

CREPES FOR CREPES TARTS

1 egg
½ cup flour
1 tablespoon sugar
½ cup milk
¼ cup cream
1 tablespoon Grand
  Marnier or Cointreau

1 teaspoon grated lemon
  peel, orange peel, or
  vanilla
1 tablespoon butter,
  melted and cooled

Beat the egg slightly and add the flour and a little milk if necessary and beat well. Add the sugar, remaining milk and cream, beating all the while. Then add the Grand Marnier or Cointreau and flavoring and the butter, melted and cooled. Let stand for at least one hour.

Butter a crepe pan or 5-inch skillet and when the butter sizzles slightly, pour in about a tablespoon and a half of batter. Watch carefully as these crepes burn more easily because of the sugar. Do not attempt to flip them; they are too delicate while they are hot. Lift up the edge of a crepe with a round-ended table knife, and if it is delicately browned turn with the fingers. Cook on the reverse side only a few seconds and turn out onto a paper towel. Stack with wax paper in between. When they are quite cold the crepes are less delicate and more manageable. Yield: 12 to 16 crepes. Any excess may be frozen.

LEMON CREPES TARTS

3 tablespoons cornstarch
1 cup sugar
1 cup boiling water
3 egg yolks
1 tablespoon butter

grated rind of 2 lemons
½ cup lemon juice
12 5-inch crepes for
    crepes tarts (page 143)

Mix cornstarch and sugar, add boiling water slowly, stir and bring to boil over low heat. Continue to boil until liquid is clear. Beat the egg yolks. Pour some of the boiling liquid over the yolks and return all the egg mixture to the pan. Cook over very low heat or over boiling water until very thick, stirring constantly, about 5 minutes. Add butter, then grated rind and lemon juice, stirring to mix well. Cool. Then fill crepes as directed on page 142 and bake for 20–25 minutes in a 300° F. oven.

ORANGE CHEESE CREPES TARTS

8 ounces cream cheese
4 tablespoons Cointreau
½ cup sugar
2 teaspoons cornstarch
1 cup orange juice

grated rind of one orange
2 egg yolks
12 5-inch crepes for
    crepes tarts (page 143)

Soften the cream cheese and beat in the Cointreau. Mix the sugar and cornstarch, add the orange juice and rind and blend well. Cook over low heat until the mixture boils and becomes clear. Cool and beat into the cream cheese mixture. Fill crepes as directed on page 133 and bake in a 300° F. oven for 30 minutes on the lowest rung. These do *not* freeze well.

CHOCOLATE CREPES TARTS

4 ounces sweet chocolate   1 teaspoon vanilla
1 tablespoon butter   1 tablespoon sugar
½ cup milk   12 5-inch crepes for
2 large eggs, separated   crepes tarts (page 143)

Melt chocolate and butter with milk over low heat, stirring to keep mixture from burning. Beat egg yolks lightly with a fork. Pour part of the hot chocolate mixture onto egg yolks then pour back and cook for another 2 minutes but do not let boil. Cool, add vanilla. Beat egg whites until they form soft peaks, add sugar gradually and beat for a few more strokes. Combine egg whites with cooled chocolate mixture. Fill crepes as directed on page 142 and bake in a 300° F. oven for 20 minutes on the lowest rung. These do *not* freeze well.

Easy Dessert Crepes with Simple Fillings

Using either plain or dessert crepes and simple fillings you can have a dessert ready in no time. For all of the following recipes the crepes, already on hand, frozen or made earlier the same day, need only to be heated in a slow oven (300° F.) for ten minutes and brought to the table in a folded napkin. Or they may be served from a chafing dish or electric skillet set at low heat. The fruit or other filling can be passed in a bowl and each person may fill his own crepes, or the hostess may, if she prefers, fill the crepes and send them around the table, passing a sauce only if there is one. The following recipes will fill 18 crepes well or as few as 12 crepes lavishly and should serve 6.

STRAWBERRY CREPES

1 quart strawberries
sugar to taste
1 cup heavy cream,

whipped, or 1 pint
vanilla ice cream
(optional)

Wash and hull the strawberries. Cut in slices and add sugar to taste. Pass plain, with whipped cream or ice cream or mix the berries with whipped cream before serving. Frozen strawberries may be used. Defrost the berries and drain off part of the juice.

Raspberries, Blackberries, Blueberries in Crepes
Using the same proportions as for Strawberry Crepes,
mix the berries with ice cream or with sweetened
whipped cream and serve as above.

Peach Crepes

6 fresh peaches   *sugar to taste*
juice of 1 lemon or lime

Peel and slice peaches. Sprinkle with lemon or lime
juice to prevent browning (and to perk up the flavor).
Add sugar to taste and let stand in the refrigerator a
few minutes before serving. Frozen or canned peaches
may be used but part of the juice of either should be
drained off. Ice cream or whipped cream may be
added.

Pineapple Crepes

1 medium pineapple   *pineapple sherbet*
sugar to taste   *(optional)*

Cut the pineapple into small slices, sugar, and let stand
in the refrigerator for at least half an hour. Serve with
pineapple sherbet. Canned pineapple may be used but
drain off part of the juice.

BANANA CREPES

6 medium or small   1 cup whipping cream
   bananas   sugar

Slice the bananas, whip the cream and sweeten to taste. Mix with the bananas and serve with crepes.

CREPES WITH PRESERVES

Apricot jam, strawberry or raspberry jam, preserved lingonberries or preisselbeeren, blackberries or peach preserves are good spread on crepes. With preisselbeeren, smaller crepes are often used and the whole crepe is spread with preserves and eaten either flat or rolled.

CREPES WITH APPLESAUCE

Pass applesauce (about 2 cups) plain or mixed with raspberries or with whipped cream with the crepes. Applesauce may be warm or cold.

CREPES WITH WALNUTS AND SUGAR

1 cup grated walnuts   *½ cup sugar*

Mix walnuts with sugar. Brush crepes with melted butter and sprinkle walnut–sugar mixture on each. The crepes should be hot rather than warm for this.

CREPES WITH WALNUTS AND WHIPPED CREAM

1 cup heavy cream   *1 cup chopped walnuts*
2 tablespoons sugar

Whip the cream with the sugar. Fold in the walnuts and pass with warm or hot crepes.

YUGOSLAVIAN CREPES WITH WALNUTS, BUTTER AND SUGAR

¼ cup butter   *1 cup grated walnuts*
¼ cup sugar

Cream butter and sugar, grate walnuts. These crepes should be hot, not merely warm, and are best filled in the kitchen. Spread a little of the butter–sugar mixture on each crepe and sprinkle with grated walnuts. Roll and put on a heated platter.

Yugoslavians are proud of their crepes which they

call Palatschinken. They sometimes serve this crepe with grated bittersweet chocolate on top of the nuts or with hot chocolate sauce over the rolled crepes.

CREPES WITH ORANGE MARMALADE AND CHOPPED PECANS

Pass 1 cup of chopped pecans along with orange marmalade.

CREPES WITH DATES AND WALNUTS IN SOUR CREAM

1 cup chopped dates   *½ cup light brown sugar*
1 cup chopped walnuts   *1 cup sour cream*

Mix the dates and walnuts together. Blend the brown sugar into the sour cream and blend the two mixtures together. Pass with warmed crepes.

Crepes with Sauces

Still easy but requiring a little more time for preparation of the filling are the recipes with a cooked sauce, served with warmed crepes.

CREPES MELBA

1 package frozen
  raspberries
2 teaspoons cornstarch
1 tablespoon water

4 fresh peaches or 1
  package frozen peaches
1 pint vanilla ice cream

Defrost raspberries and bring to a boil, stirring and mashing the berries as they cook. Mix the cornstarch with the water and add to the raspberries. Continue to cook until the liquid is clear and thickened. Peel and slice the fresh peaches and add to the raspberry sauce. If frozen peaches are used, defrost and drain before adding. Cool slightly. Serve warm with hot crepes and pass along the vanilla ice cream. Fresh or drained canned pears may be substituted.

CREPES WITH PEARS HÉLÈNE

3 fresh pears	*1 teaspoon vanilla*
1 cup water	*1 cup chocolate sauce*
¾ cup sugar	*1 pint vanilla ice cream*

Peel, core and slice pears into small pieces. Combine water and sugar and bring to a boil, slowly stirring until sugar is melted. Add sliced pears and simmer for about 3 minutes. Add the vanilla and chill the pears in the syrup. Heat chocolate sauce and pass cold pears, ice cream and hot chocolate sauce with the crepes. Since the syrup is sweet, the chocolate sauce should be almost bitter. Use less sugar in your favorite recipe.

CREPES WITH APRICOT SAUCE CZECH STYLE

2 cups apricots	*¾ cup sugar*
water to cover	*confectioner's sugar*

Cook apricots in water to cover until very soft. Press through a sieve or liquefy in a blender. Combine sugar and apricot puree and cook over low heat until thick and shiny. Spread on crepes. Sprinkle with confectioner's sugar.

CREPES WITH BUTTERSCOTCH SAUCE AND ALMONDS

1 cup light brown sugar
½ cup light corn syrup
½ cup cream
2 tablespoons butter

1 teaspoon vanilla
½ cup toasted, slivered almonds

Combine brown sugar, corn syrup and cream in a medium-sized saucepan. Bring to a boil, stirring constantly. Boil hard for 5 minutes, stirring occasionally. Remove from heat, add butter and vanilla. Stir in slivered almonds and pass with crepes.

CREPES WITH CHOCOLATE AND COCONUT

8 ounces sweet chocolate
½ cup water
1 tablespoon butter

½ cup cream (or more)
1 cup coconut (flaked type is best for this)

Melt chocolate, water and butter together. Mix in cream to make a thick sauce. Add more if necessary. Blend in the coconut and pass with crepes.

CANDY BAR CREPES

6 dessert crepes   *6 chocolate candy bars*

Wrap a crepe around each candy bar and set them in
a buttered baking pan. Bake for 15 minutes at 350° F.
If you wish, sprinkle confectioner's sugar mixed with
cocoa over the top and run under the broiler.

Crepes Suzette

Of all crepes, the ones that might have been named for a lady at the Court of Louis XIV or a little friend of Queen Victoria's aging playboy son are the most famous. Crepes Suzette deserve that fame for the delectable mixture of flavors and textures: of tart and sweet, buttery caramel and orange, delicate crepe and robust brandy, and not least for their fiery presentation. The late great chef Louis Charpentier claimed to have invented Crepes Suzette near the turn of the century for the Prince who was to be Edward VII.

If he didn't in fact invent them he certainly popularized them to the extent that there are many who think that Crepes Suzette is the generic name for all French pancakes. This recipe is not made the way M. Charpentier made his, the chief difference lying in one step. Charpentier, as do many chefs today, rubbed lump sugar over the skin of an orange to extract the flavor. We think using regular sugar and grated orange rind is not only easier but better. The following recipe is the result of long and happy experimentation.

SPECIAL CREPES FOR CREPES SUZETTE

2 eggs
¼ cup sugar
1 teaspoon grated lemon
  rind
¾ cup flour
2 tablespoons Grand
  Marnier or orange
  liqueur

1 cup half milk and
  half cream
2 tablespoons butter
  melted and cooled

Beat eggs with sugar and grated rind, mix in flour, then add Grand Marnier or orange liqueur, milk and cream and, finally, melted and cooled butter. Let stand 2 hours.

Butter a 5-inch crepe pan and when the butter bubbles up, pour in about a tablespoon and a half of batter. Tilt the pan so that batter swirls over the whole surface. Cook less than a minute on the first side. Then turn and cook for a few seconds on the other side. These are delicate pancakes and hard to handle, especially before they have set and browned. Do not try even to test them until a little brown shows at the edges.

Crepes Suzette

12 crepes for Crepes
   Suzette (page 156)
⅓ cup butter
⅓ cup sugar
grated rind of 1 orange
juice of two oranges

4 ounces of Cointreau
2 ounces Grand Marnier
3 ounces Cognac
kitchen matches
long-handled spoon

This recipe serves four which is about as many as can be served from one chafing dish or electric frying pan. With a helper you could double the recipe and each take over one pan.

Since this is to be a production, everything must be ready and at hand before you start. The crepes will have been cooked earlier, or, if frozen, thawed before they are brought to the table. The butter and sugar can be creamed together before dinner, the orange rind grated and added to them, the orange juice squeezed and the various liqueurs measured. Each should be in its own dish or glass. And don't forget the matches. Start the chafing dish or electric frying pan, bring the crepes and other ingredients in along with the plates on a tray, and then go to work with a flourish. First melt the creamed butter and sugar and let it bubble up for a minute or two. When it begins to brown add the orange juice, little by little, and the Cointreau. Cook and stir until the sauce thickens. (Have a little orange juice in reserve in case it thickens too fast.) Then take the first crepe, put it into the sauce, turn it over (using a spoon and fork or two spoons but be careful not to break it), fold it in half, then in half again. Push it to one side and repeat with the remaining crepes. Sprinkle the Grand Marnier over all.

Now for the brandy. Pour it into a large, long-handled spoon, letting some spill down over the crepes. Ask the gentleman on your right to light one of the matches and ignite the brandy in the spoon, letting it spill over onto the crepes. Swish them around so they will all get the effects of the burning brandy and try to serve the crepes (three to a person) while the flame is still burning.

SWEDISH CREPES WITH LINGONBERRIES

2 eggs	*1 cup heavy cream*
1 tablespoon sugar	*1 cup flour*
½ teaspoon salt	*confectioner's sugar*
1 cup milk	*lingonberries (preserved)*

Beat 2 eggs until light with 1 tablespoon of sugar and ½ teaspoon salt. Gradually add 1 cup of milk and 1 cup of cream alternately with one cup of flour. Let stand covered for two hours, then beat lightly. The best way to cook these crepes is in a special Swedish griddle with round depressions to receive the thin dough. However, some practice will help you achieve a fairly accurate 2-inch round (proper size). The technique is to drop the batter from a teaspoon, twirling it slowly. Several crepes can be cooked in the same pan once you have caught on. But it might be easier to use a small pan for each crepe to begin with. The pan, as always, should be clean. A small amount of butter is put into it and when it bubbles up but has not started to brown, lower the heat and drop your tea-spoonful of batter into it. Turn with a spatula and brown on the other side. Keep the crepes warm in a slow oven as you continue to cook them. Just before serving sprinkle with confectioner's sugar. Usually four or five are served on a dessert plate arranged around a spoonful of lingonberries.

Yield: about four dozen.

BAKED CREPES

Baked crepes are mostly Scandinavian or German in origin and are either baked in large heavy skillets (with burnproof handles) or in flat tins. The Scandi-navian baked pancakes are usually made of more deli-cate batter than the German ones. Usually they contain a filling such as strawberries, apples, peaches or lingonberries or preisselbeeren—these last two can be bought in jars and cut in wedges. Sometimes if they are spread thin enough, the filling is put on top and they are rolled up, covered with powdered sugar and set aflame with kirsch or some other liqueur or brandy, and sliced into serving portions.

CREPES SOUFFLÉ NORMANDIE

4 eggs separated
¼ cup sugar
¾ cup flour
1 cup milk

1 tablespoon lemon juice
or apple brandy or
calvados

Beat egg yolks and sugar together until thick, add flour gradually. The mixture will be stiff. Then add milk in small amounts, beating thoroughly between each addition until mixture is smooth. Cover and let stand while making filling. After filling is precooked beat egg whites until stiff but still shiny. Mix a quarter of the egg whites thoroughly into the egg yolk mixture then cut the rest in gently with a flexible spatula, folding over and over. Meanwhile butter and heat two large ovenproof skillets or a baking pan 10 or 12 by 14 to 16 inches either on top of the stove or in an oven set at 350° F. When the pans are hot, pour in half the crepe mixture, then the filling, then the rest of the crepe mixture. Bake at 350° F. about 30 minutes.

FILLING

2 medium apples, peeled,
cored and cut into thin
slices
1 tablespoon butter
juice of half a lemon

¼ cup sugar (more if
apples are tart)
1 teaspoon cinnamon
(other spices can be
added or substituted)

Melt butter in skillet and sauté apple slices on low heat. When they begin to soften, add lemon juice and sugar and continue cooking until almost tender. Pour off and save excess juices. When crepe is baked, pour juices over top and bring to table immediately. Although this is like a soufflé, it does not fall much, is good cold and can be frozen and reheated.

VARIATIONS

CREPE SOUFFLÉ WITH PEACHES
Use 3 or 4 peaches. Peel, slice and cook the same as apples for Crepes Soufflé Normandie, but do not add cinnamon.

CREPES SOUFFLÉ WITH STRAWBERRIES OR RASPBERRIES
Use a pint of strawberries or raspberries. Sweeten to taste, but do not precook. Proceed the same as for Crepes Soufflé Normandie.

BAKED ROLLED CREPES

These should be poured not more than a ½-inch thick. Use either Crepes Soufflé Normandie (page 160) or Sweet Souffléed Baked Crepes (page 33). Sprinkle a little granulated sugar over the top of the crepes and bake until puffy and well browned on top. Spread with any desired fruit filling, and roll up in the pan using two spoons to nudge it along. Sprinkle with confectioner's sugar or pour warm brandy or liqueur over the top and set aflame. Cut into serving pieces at the table.

CREPES CRÈME PRALINE

Use any of the pastry creams in the chapter on sauces (pages 176–177). Melt a half cup of sugar over low heat. Add a handful of almonds. Stir until the sugar liquefies and turns caramel color and the almonds brown. Turn into a large pan and when it is cool, pulverize in a blender, grinder or mortar. Use 3 or 4 tablespoons to flavor the cream. Pass with warmed crepes. Or fill and roll crepes in a buttered baking dish, sprinkle more of the praline on top, and put under a hot broiler until glazed, about 5 minutes. Use plain crepes, dessert crepes or cocoa crepes. This freezes well and needs no defrosting before baking.

ALTERNATE FILLING

CREPES PRALINE WITH APRICOT JAM
Along with the praline, blend 3 or 4 tablespoons of thick apricot jam into the pastry cream. Use plain, dessert or cocoa crepes.

CREPES FRANGIPANE WITH BRANDY

1 recipe pastry cream (page 176)	1 tablespoon brandy confectioner's sugar
4 or 5 crushed macaroons	16–18 plain or dessert
1 tablespoon grated orange rind	crepes

Add the crushed macaroons, grated orange rind and brandy to the pastry cream. Put a spoonful or two down the center of each crepe, roll and place seam side down in a buttered baking dish. Sprinkle with confectioner's sugar and put under a hot broiler to glaze, 5 minutes or less. This freezes well and needs no defrosting before baking.

STACKED DESSERT CREPES

Crepes for dessert can be stacked in layers with different fillings in between and either glazed under the broiler or baked. Two or three fillings can be used and sauce passed to put over the top if desired. Since dessert crepes are extremely delicate and hard to bake, either use plain crepes or do not make them more than 6 inches in diameter. Four or five 6-inch crepes with fillings in between will serve 3 to 4 if the fillings are rich. Plain and cocoa crepes can be alternated. Try chocolate and plain pastry cream with various flavorings. Ice cream or flavored whipped cream can be used if the top layer is fruit or pastry cream and the

stacked crepes are run under the broiler for only a
minute or two.

KAISERSCHMARREN

12–14 crepes, plain, main   ½ cup raisins soaked in
   course or dessert   rum or cut up candied
4 tablespoons butter   fruit
½ cup sugar   ½ teaspoon cinnamon
½ cup slivered toasted   (optional)
   almonds

Cut or tear the crepes into pieces. Melt the butter in a
large skillet, add the shredded crepes, sugar, toasted
almonds and raisins or candied fruit. Stir and toss until
all the crepe bits are coated but the sugar is not
melted. Sprinkle with cinnamon if desired.

The exact translation of *schmarren* is uncertain; the
Emperor's Pancakes is the most formal; some have suggested the Emperor's Mess, or the Emperor's Foolish-
ness as a proper translation. It really doesn't matter.
What does matter is that while no one who isn't as
foolish as a Kaiser would tear up perfectly good crepes
to make this mélange, it is a perfectly wonderful way
to use the mangled crepes that result when pans aren't
well seasoned or tyros are learning to flip. Freeze what
mistakes you can't resist eating then and there and
when you've accumulated enough, be an Emperor and
have your fancy!

Crepes for Breakfast

Any of the simpler dessert crepes, those spread with jelly or jam or berries, make a good breakfast crepe. Plain or dessert crepes can be simply spread with butter and sugar or butter and honey, maple sugar or light brown sugar. Orange crepes (page 141) are also a good item for breakfast as are any of the baked dessert crepes. Crepes with eggs may seem a little redundant but unlike omelets they can be prepared ahead of time and are thus a good idea for a crowd at either a regular morning or after-the-party breakfast. The possibilities, of course, are legion, but here are a few suggestions.

CREPES WITH SCRAMBLED EGGS AND BACON

8 eggs   6 strips bacon
2 tablespoons butter   12 crepes
salt and pepper to taste   extra butter
2 tablespoons cream

Beat the eggs lightly. Melt the butter and over low heat scramble the eggs until they are just set but not dry, stirring all the time. Salt and pepper to taste and stir in the cream off heat. Meanwhile fry or broil the bacon until it is crisp and crumble it.

Put a spoonful of the scrambled eggs down the center of each crepe, sprinkle with a bit of crumbled bacon. Roll and place seam side down in a buttered baking dish. Brush with a little melted butter and put in a 350° F. oven for 10 minutes if freshly made or for 15 minutes if they have been held in the refrigerator.

VARIATIONS

CREPES WITH SCRAMBLED EGGS AND HAM
Substitute a few slices of frizzled thinly sliced boiled ham for the bacon.

CREPES WITH SCRAMBLED EGGS AND CHEESE
Add cheddar or American cheese to the eggs while they are cooking and sprinkle more cheese over the top of the crepes before baking.

CREPES BENEDICT
Put a slice of Canadian bacon on top of the scrambled eggs in each crepe, top with Hollandaise sauce. Roll and spread tops of crepes with more Hollandaise sauce.

CREPES WITH SCRAMBLED EGGS AND VARIOUS FILLINGS
Most of the chicken fillings and many of the seafood fillings in this book will combine well with eggs to make an elegant dish for brunch or late supper rather than breakfast. The recipes should be cut in half to serve 6 with 2 crepes apiece in combination with 8 eggs.

CREPES WITH SAUSAGES

For 12 crepes, fry 12 sausages until cooked. Wrap a crepe around each sausage and serve immediately.

CREPES WITH SCRAMBLED EGGS SPANISH STYLE

8 eggs
4 tablespoons butter
1 cup chopped tomatoes
¼ cup chopped celery
¼ cup chopped green
   pepper

½ cup chopped onions
2 tablespoons cream
salt and pepper to taste
12 crepes

Melt 2 tablespoons of the butter in a large skillet and sauté the chopped onions, celery and green pepper until limp. Add the chopped tomatoes which have been drained and cook over high heat for 2 or 3 minutes until mixture thickens. Beat the eggs lightly and scramble in the rest of the butter, not allowing eggs to become dry. Remove from heat and beat in 2 tablespoons of cream.

Put a spoonful of egg mixture down the center of each crepe, top with a spoonful of vegetable mixture. Roll and turn seam side down in a buttered baking dish. Bake for 10 minutes at 350° F. if freshly made, for 15 minutes if held in the refrigerator. Do *not* freeze.

Stocks
and
Sauces

*A good chicken or beef stock can add a great deal to a sauce
and a good sauce is the making of many crepes fillings. Although some of the recipes in this book include sauces made
right in the pan with the basic ingredients, others call for a
finished sauce. If you have a cream sauce, a tomato sauce,
a brown sauce or any of the more complicated sauces built
on these or your own, use it by all means. But for young
cooks or cooks who are dissatisfied with their present recipes, here are a few.*

BROWN STOCK

2 *pounds beef from shin, plate or chuck*	*few sprigs parsley*
2–3 *pounds beef or veal bones (including marrow bones)*	1 *teaspoon salt*
	2 *quarts water*
1 *onion, quartered*	*optional seasonings:*
2 *carrots, cut in large pieces*	1 *clove garlic*
	¼ *teaspoon thyme*
1 *large stalk celery with tops*	1 *bay leaf*

Brown meat and bones, onion and carrots in a roasting pan in a 400° F. oven for about 30 minutes. Transfer browned meat and vegetables to a large kettle, at least 4-quart capacity. Add celery, parsley and optional seasonings. Rinse out roasting pan with part of the water, getting up all the browned particles, and pour over the meat and vegetables along with the rest of the water. Bring just to the simmer and simmer for 4 hours. Strain the stock into another kettle. If it is to be used immediately, skim off the fat with a spoon or bulb skimmer. Otherwise chill and remove fat after it solidifies. Store in containers in freezer or refrigerate, boiling up every 4 days. Part of stock can be frozen in ice trays and the cubes stored in plastic bags so that small amounts of stock can be used to enrich sauces and gravies.

Notes on stock: A larger amount of meat can be cooked and then taken out while it still has flavor enough to be used for other purposes. If stock is not strong enough it can be boiled rapidly until the flavor has become more concentrated.

CHICKEN STOCK

1 *large fryer*	1 *carrot*
(or stewing chicken)	1 *stalk celery*
2 *pounds chicken backs,*	*parsley*
wings and giblets	1 *teaspoon salt*
1 *onion*	

Clean and cut up chicken. Put chicken, backs, wings and giblets in a large kettle with the onion, carrot and celery, cut in large pieces. Add parsley, salt and 2 quarts cold water. Bring to the simmer and simmer for half an hour. Remove chicken breasts, bone when cooled and return skin and bones to the kettle. Simmer half an hour longer and remove legs and thighs. Return bones and skin to kettle and simmer for another hour. Cool and remove fat from top. Refrigerate or freeze in containers or ice cube trays.

Notes on chicken stock: French chefs usually add thyme (¼ teaspoon dried). We consider it better to add the thyme in particular recipes and leave it out of the basic stock. If you can get stewing chickens the stock may simmer longer for each step. For many of the recipes using chicken in this book, the stock is made while cooking the chicken for the crepe filling. However, there are some recipes which use raw chicken for an ingredient and for these a little chicken stock is good to have on hand.

MEDIUM CREAM SAUCE

3 *tablespoons butter*
3 *tablespoons flour*
2 *cups milk, stock or*
  half of each

½ *cup heavy cream*
salt and pepper to taste

Melt butter, add flour and stir with a wooden spoon until well mixed and bubbly, but do not let mixture brown. Heat milk, stock or combination of the two to simmer point. Remove bubbling flour and butter from heat, pour in all the boiling liquid at once and stir vigorously. Return to heat and simmer for ten or fifteen minutes, stirring to prevent scorching. Add cream bit by bit and stir to blend.

If instant flour is used, mix all the ingredients except the cream together in saucepan, blend well and heat to simmer point. Simmer for 10–15 minutes, stirring well.

This is a medium-thick sauce. If it is too thick, thin with milk, stock or wine, if you like.

THICK CREAM SAUCE

Use 4 tablespoons flour and 4 tablespoons butter. Make the same as Medium Cream Sauce. This is too thick to use as a top sauce. However it is a good sauce to add to fillings which have some unthickened liquid. And, of course, it can be thinned by adding extra milk or extra stock, but use up to a half cup for each cup of sauce.

ENRICHED CREAM SAUCE

Add one egg yolk with the cream for each cup of sauce. If thick sauce is used it should be thinned before adding egg yolk, which itself is a thickener.

CREAM SAUCE WITH CORNSTARCH AS THICKENING

2 cups milk or half stock   ½ cup cream
    and half milk   2 tablespoons butter
2 tablespoons cornstarch   salt and pepper to taste

Mix a little of the milk or stock with the cornstarch to a smooth paste. Heat the rest to near boiling and stir in the cornstarch paste. Simmer for about 10 minutes until sauce is well thickened, add the cream and simmer until the sauce thickens again. Add the cream bit by bit. Just before using beat in the butter.

This sauce may be enriched with eggs beaten up with the cream; wine may be added and cooked down, also grated cheese may be added.

MORNAY SAUCE (SIMPLE)

Add 2 tablespoons white wine, one egg yolk and ¼ cup cream for each cup of Medium Cream Sauce. Stir in 2 tablespoons or more of Parmesan, or Parmesan and Swiss cheese, grated.

SPECIAL MORNAY SAUCE

2 tablespoons finely
chopped shallots or
onions
2 tablespoons finely
chopped carrot
2 tablespoons finely
chopped celery
2 tablespoons finely
chopped ham
6 tablespoons butter

6 tablespoons flour
3 cups of half milk and
half chicken stock or
bouillon
¾ cup white wine
3 egg yolks
1 cup cream
1½ cups grated Parmesan
and Swiss cheese
salt and pepper to taste

The vegetables and ham must all be very finely chopped—really minced. Melt the butter in a heavy saucepan and when it bubbles stew the vegetables and ham for at least 15 minutes, preferably half an hour, but do not let butter brown. Add the flour and stir and cook for another five minutes. Heat the milk and stock and off heat pour into the mixture, stirring vigorously. Add the white wine and simmer for 10–15 minutes. Beat the egg yolks with the cream and add off heat, stirring vigorously. If the sauce is to be used for a filling, the vegetables may be left in. If it is to be used as a top sauce, strain them out. Just before using, stir in the grated cheese and check for salt and pepper.

QUICK BLENDER HOLLANDAISE SAUCE

¼ pound butter
(one stick)
3 egg yolks

2 tablespoons lemon juice
¼ teaspoon salt
pinch of pepper

Melt butter to bubbling, being careful that it does not brown. Place egg yolks, lemon juice, salt and pepper in a blender jar. Turn on blender and add hot butter in droplets very slowly. Blend only a few seconds until sauce is thick and smooth. Correct seasonings.

EVELYN'S FRESH TOMATO SAUCE

8 tomatoes

3 tablespoons butter

For approximately 3 cups of sauce use 8 fresh ripe tomatoes. Chop them into chunks and cook them uncovered in a heavy saucepan with no liquid until they cook to a thick pulp. When thick, stir in about 3 tablespoons butter which helps to smooth the sauce.

When cooking you may also add: 1 bay leaf, 1 tablespoon grated onion, choice of any herbs such as basil, thyme, oregano.

VANILLA PASTRY CREAM

1½ cups milk	5 tablespoons flour
½-inch piece vanilla bean	4 egg yolks
or 1 teaspoon vanilla	2 tablespoons butter
¼ cup sugar	

Heat the milk to just under boiling with the vanilla bean. While it is heating, combine sugar and flour and then add egg yolks and beat until well mixed. Pour the hot milk over the egg mixture slowly, stirring rapidly with a wire whisk or if the pan is Teflon, with a wooden spoon. Cook over very low heat or in a double boiler stirring continuously until the cream is very thick—about 5 minutes. Do not allow to boil. Stir in the butter and the vanilla extract if vanilla bean was not used. (Discard vanilla bean if it was used.) Stir occasionally to prevent skin from forming. Or only stir in half the butter and dot the top with the rest to keep skin from forming.

VARIATIONS

CHOCOLATE PASTRY CREAM

This is made the same as vanilla pastry cream except that 1 tablespoon of flour can be omitted because the chocolate acts as a thickening agent. Use 3 ounces of semisweet chocolate and stir in while the cream is still hot. Or use 2 squares of bitter or baking chocolate; in which case, increase sugar to ½ cup.

Light Pastry Cream

Beat 2 to 4 egg whites until stiff and add 1 to 2 table-spoons of sugar, beating well afterward. Fold into either plain or chocolate pastry cream. With plain cream this is sometimes called Cream St. Honoré.

Rich Pastry Cream

Add up to 1 cup of whipped cream to either plain or chocolate pastry cream. Whip the cream with a little sugar.

Rich Light Pastry Cream

Use both egg whites and whipped cream, folding in together with either plain or Chocolate Pastry Cream.

Other Flavors and Additions

Up to 1 cup of chopped nuts may be added to any cream; or ¼ cup of pulverized praline (sugar and almonds or hazelnuts cooked until sugar melts and turns caramel colored).

Also up to a quarter of a pound of pulverized stale macaroons or almond paste. This is called Frangipane.

Creams may be flavored with brandy, strong coffee, rum or liqueurs—up to 2 tablespoons.

HOT CHOCOLATE SAUCE

6 ounces semisweet   2 tablespoons cognac,
  chocolate   rum, or coffee
heavy cream

Melt chocolate over hot water. Stir in enough heavy
cream to smooth and blend thoroughly. Add cognac,
brandy, rum, or coffee for extra flavoring.

Index